THE STUDENT AND HIS STUDIES

The Student and
His Studies

BY

ESTHER RAUSHENBUSH

Wesleyan University Press

MIDDLETOWN, CONNECTICUT

Copyright © 1964 by Wesleyan University

Library of Congress Catalog Card Number: 64–22376
Manufactured in the United States of America
First Edition

To Carl

Contents

Foreword

RECENT discussion of the education of college students, in both professional and popular writing, is based on two largely unrelated assumptions. One reflects the concern of scholars and teachers with the acquisition of knowledge, methods of instruction, training and research. The other reflects the psychologist's preoccupation with the emotional aspects of personality. The first largely ignores the tremendous effect individual differences among students have on the way their studies are assimilated and used in their development. The second obscures the intellectual component of growth, largely ignoring the influence of the curriculum, and pays attention principally to personal relationships and activities outside the classroom.

The Hazen Foundation has undertaken to explore connections between these two concerns with education, and this book is the first fruit of that undertaking. The study began with curiosity as to what might be confidently affirmed relative to the influence of the curriculum, reading, writing, and the rest of the central business of higher education upon the development of students. It was conceived as a quest for evidence and ideas.

For this inquiry the primary qualifications were those of a successful, experienced teacher, sensitive to student development, and the author brought these qualities in rich measure to the undertaking. After seven years of teaching literature at Barnard College and Columbia University, she went to Sarah Lawrence College to participate in the development of experimental programs. These are reflected in her book *Literature for Individual Education* and another, of which she was co-author and co-editor, titled *Achievement in the College Years*. After eleven years of teaching she was dean during the period when a graduate studies program and a teacher training program were developed, as well as a joint summer program with New York University for prospective college teachers. This experience with both faculty and students opened many opportunities for consultation in other colleges and universities. The focal point was always the effort to make the learning experience of undergraduates a vital matter, and education was conceived as directed toward that end.

As a first step it was proposed to interview a relatively small number of students in different kinds of liberal arts colleges. The author concentrated her inquiries in eight colleges, enlisting friends and educators in identifying students whose studies seemed central to their growth and change. How students were selected for interviewing is told in the Author's Preface. Interviews extended over a period of many months, during which she read the students' papers and essays and corresponded with them. She has reflected long upon these experiences and formulated various implications for college educators based upon them.

The heart of this book is the biographies of four students, showing the various ways that literature, the study of science or of politics, and discussion of these matters with teachers, friends, and fellow students, actually contributed in crucial ways to their lives. The names are pseudonyms, but each student has read the biography and approved its use here. Each of these situations suggested a particular topic for further inquiry, and these have been developed in related chapters which follow each biography. These reflect the author's intimate acquaintance with all the other students with whom she conferred, and her wider experience as well. To be sure, other types of situations and influences might be studied and would undoubtedly prove illuminating. It is hoped that this offering may be stimulating to teachers and other educators, and lead to wider recognition of the vital significance of the intellectual work of students.

The Hazen Foundation wishes to express its sincere appreciation to Esther Raushenbush for the concerned and imaginative way she has conducted this study during the past two years, and also to thank all who have worked with her.

— PAUL J. BRAISTED
The Hazen Foundation

An Acknowledgment

EARLY in my life as a teacher, my colleagues in the administration and faculty of Sarah Lawrence College revealed to me by example how much more there is to know about a student's accomplishment than a grade-point average can tell. This made all the difference, and it marks my largest indebtedness.

In the present search, I enjoyed most and learned most from the students who gave me so much of their time, who talked with me about their college work, its satisfactions and frustrations. I am grateful to them for that, and for their interest in the explorations that led to this book. My special indebtedness to the four whose academic histories are told here is obvious.

Every college and university I visited for interviews with students received me generously, and many people helped me find the students I wanted to talk with, and the information I needed to have about them and about the institution. I cannot name them here, because there were so many of them; but I hope they know I am grateful, and I hope, if they see this book, they will not feel their time and interest were ill spent.

David Riesman's circumstantial knowledge of education in American colleges, of the American society in which education takes place, of students he has taught and talked with, were important to me, and I thank him especially for the time and wisdom he gave to reading and commenting on the manuscript.

Paul Braisted, of the Hazen Foundation, and Max Wise, suggested the design of this study. Professor Wise knew of my long association with students, one by one, in my own college, and urged me to learn about other students by talking with them. I owe him much for his comments on the manuscript.

The Hazen Foundation invited me to take time to seek out students whose academic life had been important to them, and to listen to what they had to say about it. It was a welcome invitation — an assignment pleasing after many years of thinking about this subject. The gift of time the Foundation provided puts me much in its debt. Even more important was Paul Braisted's conviction that education should indeed be designed to be a lively and serious experience, and his faith that many students will respond when it is; his interest in what I was doing, and his encouragement; and the conversations we had, about education and about the students and their colleges, in the course of the two years this project has been under way. For all this I thank him and the Hazen Foundation.

—E. R.

Author's Preface

THERE is a character in *Lord Jim,* a Bavarian trader and butterfly collector named Stein, who describes the inescapable effort of every man's life as the effort to discover "how to be."

"We want in so many different ways to be. This magnificent butterfly finds a little heap of dirt and sits still on it; but man he will never on his heap of mud keep still. He want to be so, and again he want to be so."

And so he tries, in the face of hazards in and outside himself, to learn to live with ideas and actions, persons and events, that draw him in to life, as he seeks to discover himself at last.

In the college years, a time of heightened consciousness, students seek such self-knowledge. Sometimes their studies are remote and help little or not at all in the effort. Sometimes they are a powerful force.

During the course of a year, in 1962 and 1963, I visited campuses in several parts of the country to talk with students about their work. I was interested in students who had become involved, or engaged, in their intellectual life, so that it mattered seriously to them. I did not seek out the remarkably talented few, whose qualities and gifts set them apart from others; the students who appear here are like many other intelligent young people whose education makes a difference in their lives — who use their education as a means of growing up.

If we judge successful use of the college years by the usual academic measures, it is easy to find the students who make the most of those years. The "best" students, by those measures, are on the dean's list, and they make Phi Beta Kappa in their junior year. But many students of the sort who interested me are not on these lists; nor do all the students who are on them fit the criteria I find important. Often students who are deeply involved in their education do not get straight A's; and we all know students for whom A's come easy, or who get high grades out of compulsion, or ambition, or parental pressure, or fear, or the wish to be honored, who never do become engaged in their intellectual life.

I wanted to find students who pursued questions, who were not always asking for answers, whose education was not only the acquisition of knowledge, but a process of inquiry, whether about ideas or art or actions or about the prospects for the future — personal, national, religious, or philosophical.

How can we know, by looking at the record of a student's grades, how he used the learning he was engaged in — the reading and the lectures and the talk? How, if at all, did his studies help turn a detached, unmotivated boy into a student? What happens when students are intent on developing talents already obvious, have no time for exploration that may reveal others? What happens when we encourage exploration? What do able and interested students say about teaching and their teachers? About their own attachment or failure of attachment to the events of the world they are growing up in? About how their ideas of what to do, and what they must learn, consolidate or change in the course of the years? Can we know anything about what the study of science or literature or philosophy has meant to a particular person in the process of his inquiry?

The students in this book entered college in 1958 or 1959, and graduated in 1962 or 1963. I talked at length with about 170 of them — 15 or 25 on each campus — talks that lasted between an hour and two hours each; with many of them a second time, after an interval of some weeks or months, and with some of them from time to time through the year. They gave me papers they had written, other evidence of work they had done that bore on the things they said about their education, wrote me letters. I came to know some of them quite well. Most of them were juniors when I first met them; I saw some again as seniors, a few after they had finished college.

That year of talking with them was a year of tremendous events in this country and in the world, and it followed a decade of unprecedented political change, scientific advance, and social revolution, violent and peaceful. It also followed a decade of intensive critical examination of education, especially of the attitudes, values, accomplishments, and promise of students in college. Scores of people, particularly during the last half of the 1950s, had been writing with indignation or despair about the indifference and incompetence of students: They lived on the surface, seeking to understand neither themselves nor their surroundings; they were ignorant of many things they needed to know in order to cope with the modern world; they had little interest in ideas; they were scientifically illiterate; they were self-centered and had no concern for public affairs or for leading, or even for participating, in the changes that were taking place in society and that would call for educated leadership and participation.

This book is not written to refute the evidence that led to that despairing judgment. Writing it started with the knowledge that many college students were concerned, not indifferent, and that their college education seemed to foster their concern. It has been written out of an interest in seeing how this happened, by following the academic history of such students, by exploring the circumstances and the educational experiences that helped create their values, by considering what in their academic life advanced and what hindered their education.

We often talk about what we, as educators, think students "need" in education; and *they* talk, too, about what they think they need. I was interested to observe under what conditions students found it possible to search out their needs, and to seek to satisfy them through their studies.

I was interested in students who were trying to develop competence; who had, or were seeking, a sense of worth through understanding themselves and their present or possible achievements; students for whom intellectual life was an instrument of growth.

A number of observations repeated themselves in the course of what was not research, but search: For one thing, most of the students I talked with — not all of them — did have, in some terms, an interest in public affairs, some an intense interest. In a few cases this was stimulated by the general climate of the institution, or efforts of the college to encourage it by the structure of the curriculum. But in most cases these students did not find such stimulus in the atmosphere, in what Clark Kerr calls the "animating spirit" of the institution. They either came with an interest, or found it in extracurricular activities, or it was brought out by some professor who was himself concerned with the events of the world, and concerned with involving his students. When we despair about the political indifference of our students it also makes sense to consider what we do to banish indifference. I have commented on these matters in my chapter on "Public and Private Purposes," and in other places in the book.

It early became evident that many of these able students were extraordinarily ignorant about science. Most of them reported that they "had had science" but had not brought away enough to help them understand, even dimly, the catastrophic changes that are taking place in scientific knowledge of the physical universe. Many had found the study of science routine and unilluminating. A few dedicated science students found their way to teachers and programs that set them on the road to understanding, but most of the students did not. I have said something about their experience in "In and Out of Science."

One thing that emerged from this study was the evidence of how education advanced when an institution seemed to fit, or suit, the needs of a particular student. This is not, in the sense I mean it, a matter of higher or lower academic standards, but a matter of whether or not the talents, the personal qualities, the developing intellectual bent of a student and the design or quality of the institution seemed to be especially congenial. Large-scale studies of the character or climate of institutions have been made and others are under way; and these will throw much more light on this issue than my story can do. But close observation of some individual histories also indicates the importance of this factor in an educational system that is undertaking to provide for a larger and more diverse company of students than has ever been conceived of before. It seemed to me, as I have indicated in her story, that Margaret Weaver attended a college that suited her admirably. She would probably have done well elsewhere, too, but the circumstances her college provided were fortunate for her. Alex Rovere was even more fortunate — elsewhere he might have been lost to any education at all.

Among the scores of things these students said about their teachers, one of the most important was the great spur it was to them when they had a sense that a teacher was really sharing his experience with them in some serious way. While many of them established and cherished good personal relations with teachers, this experience of communication was important whether their association was personal or impersonal; and it existed in the relation of teachers to students in individual conferences, in discussion groups, and in large lecture classes. Whatever language the students found for speaking of it, what counted was the teacher's communication, not only of knowledge but of his own commitment — a quality that gave students the sense that they and the teacher were occupying the same world. I have tried to say something about this in the story of Anna Warren's education, and in the chapter on teachers.

And, finally, one of the most illuminating experiences, in coming to know the history of students in some detail, was to see what I have called the internal shape of their education. The student's "major" defines his education in only a limited, however useful, way. What seems more important to me is how often his studies give his life and thought a particular bent or quality, or bring that quality to light; how often his attention, whatever he is studying, turns more and more clearly to particular questions to pursue, or to particular ways of thinking, or to particular ideas or beliefs to follow. Whatever starts him seeking, he then seeks after that in whatever he studies.

I found such designs many times; and many times, after several long interviews with a student, after he had talked about the work he had done from the beginning, about papers he had written that he had given me to read, he said, "I have never had a chance to see it all together this way before." I think one does not know whether an education has such a form until one knows a student's work quite well.

We sometimes characterize a student by the profession he is preparing for, what he has learned to do, the content of knowledge he has acquired. In these respects his studies give an external shape to his education. But this external shape only partly revealed what I needed to know — the inner shape of his education, how his studies were serving him in the process of learning to *be,* to what extent the kind of individual he was trying to become had been influenced by a course in literature or a course in history. As a student's bent develops, it in turn influences his choice of what to study. He seeks out certain teachers, when he has the chance, for what they are as well as for what they know. The particular slant of a paper he writes reveals something about where he is in his process of becoming.

Striking differences among students can be hidden by superficial likenesses — and the professor may never know the difference. Two students may have like College Entrance examination scores; like grade-point averages; the same majors; similar electives. They may look alike in all these ways, and so belong to the same statistical categories — and still be having experiences with education so different as to need describing in altogether different language.

How did I find the kind of students I was seeking? In most of the places, I knew somebody who would understand what I was looking for. In the first college I went to I was given a hundred questionnaires to read, selected at random. They were detailed and revealing; they had been filled out at the end of the freshman year by students in a special program for freshmen. Those freshmen had become juniors when I saw their questionnaires. I selected twenty that read as though something intellectually valuable had happened in that freshman year, and I asked these students if they would talk with me about their work.

In another college I met first with a group of a dozen major and minor administrators, and we talked most of a day about the values I was interested in discovering in their students. Some of the people there understood at once. Others started listing students because they were in honors seminars, or had the highest grade-point averages; and when I explained that such a list would not necessarily give the evidence I wanted, one administrator said, "This makes me uneasy — I never thought of students quite the way you're thinking about them."

In one college four or five people who dealt with students in quite different capacities all made out independent lists of students they thought were using their education creatively and when names appeared several times I chose those students to talk with.

Students were left as free as possible to decide whether to talk with me or not, and were never followed up if they chose not to come. Usually I wrote to them, told them what I was interested in, said I would be in the neighborhood at a certain time, and invited them to make appointments if they were interested. Almost all of them came. Of those twenty whose questionnaires I had originally selected, in the college I first went to, seventeen made appointments. One of the others was in a hospital; one of the other two called me when I made a second visit to the campus and said, "I didn't have an interview when you were here last. Could I now?" The twentieth I never heard from.

In another college — the only one in which this happened — more than a third of the students made no response to my notes, and all but two of those who did come were girls. Later I asked about it. The first explanation I got was that the boys were busy. But I didn't think that was it; boys on other campuses were busy, too. What came out later — and it fitted my other observations there, the feel of the place, the things students said — was that there was a habit among students of being on guard there. More on guard than in most places.

I have written about four different students. Why these? I chose them because I found that they had responded in interesting and sometimes moving ways to their education, as students often do. These four illustrate how different are the needs of students, and how these different needs determine their use of the subject matter of college education; and yet each has many counterparts in almost any kind of college. The four differ from each other in ways that descriptions of majors, grades, or test scores do not reveal; and these usual measures by which we judge students would not reveal, either, the likeness of these four to others I talked with and did not write about. Perhaps these accounts of individual histories will remind us to seek, from time to time, ways of understanding the education of college students in addition to those we commonly use.

None of the students whose stories are in this book is "ideal"; no education described here accomplished all I wish it had; none is a model for anyone else to follow. But for all of them, and many like them, the experience of study and learning, the intellectual life, the chance for thought and judgment, and for developing values by which to design their lives, has started them on the road to the discovery of how to be.

PART ONE

Cases and Circumstances

I

Scott Hansen at Harvard

As one talks with one student after another, trying to find out how each one is using his education, the most enduring subject for reflection, it seems to me, is how much and in what ways his studies are knitted into the fabric of his life and thought — both into his intellectual growth and into the successive resolutions of his beliefs, partial and temporary though such resolutions may be. How much is what he learns an instrument of daily use as he grows up, and how much does it lie out there, a stored and more-or-less valuable possession, perhaps to be useful later, but often not needed for use now?

All students in these college years are, one way or another, absorbed in the process of growth. How conscious they are of their absorption varies immensely from one to another, and the quality or character of the absorption varies too.

Sometimes, when an outsider reviews the education of a student, what stands out is what he has studied and how his knowledge has grown. One sees whether and how his intellectual power has increased, his judgment deepened; how direction for future work has become clearer; how he slowly surrounds himself, by means of what he learns, with assets and acquisitions on which he can draw, now and later, in fashioning his life. This learning can be serious and important. It is prominent because it has an objective, solid quality. It is described by describing what the individual has been learning, what he knows, how he works, and how he thinks. The story of Margaret Weaver is such a case.

But sometimes what stands out is not what a student has studied so much as what he was and what he is becoming. However intense the intellectual concerns may be, however serious the acquisition of knowledge, one has the impression with some students that these experiences are not simply stored up, acquisitions, possessions, but rather that they daily flow into the life of the individual and daily affect its design and direction.

But the student involved in the development of his own convictions and beliefs is also concerned with subject matter; and the student involved mainly in the acquisition of knowledge *may* be concerned with values or beliefs. When the education of a student is directed conspicuously toward one or the other, an account of his experience may illuminate not only the impact of his education on him, but the impact of education on other students.

Scott Hansen's story is here because his is a lively instance of an education in which learning is taken in and churned and absorbed and so becomes assimilated into the life of the person. Scott Hansen did not always have his mind on his work. In a sense, his mind was not on his work at all, through most of his undergraduate years. From the time he began to discover that he had to know who he was, and what he was up to, his mind was always on *that* and he used what he read and studied and wrote (when he *did* use it) in the service of his discovery. "The idea of trying to know yourself was foreign to me before Harvard," he wrote at the end of his freshman year.

The most important part of this effort to know himself, and therefore the most important part of the story of his education, is a slowly increasing breadth of inquiry and a slowly growing objectivity from the first to the fourth year of college. The account of his history that follows is an attempt to describe his use of his education in the process.

He Would Be a Math Student

THE process of conscious development began with a sudden revolution in Scott's idea of what his college education was for. The revolution took place early in his freshman year and quite changed the direction of his studies, causing him to abandon the work he thought he had come to Harvard to do:

> Where did Harvard begin? It was a "highest-hope" school which I saw little prospect of attending when I applied. I had been pleased that the area Harvard Club was interested in me, and the pamphlet, "An Introduction to Harvard College" . . . gave me the quite favorable impression that Harvard was an earnest, serious and yet alive, college. Just after being delighted with getting a Harvard regional scholarship (which made Harvard financially possible), I visited Harvard for two days, living in a frosh dorm. The over-all impression I received of daily Yard life sold me, and I went home talking. I came to Harvard with no specific expectations, but excitement and hard work. I think I was very receptive

and eager, partly because I had been getting very tired of high school.

Scott came to Harvard expecting to be a mathematics student. He was studying mathematics in high school during the middle fifties, when high school teaching, and especially the teaching of mathematics and science, trembled under attacks from those who knew what was wrong with American education, and from those who did not. To spur the gifted, to rescue talent, to make bright students learn more and learn it better and faster, was the new educational task.

There was in Scott's high school a mathematics teacher who seems to have had a special genius, and also a group of students on whom she could use her gifts. They did more and more, and better and better, work in mathematics. They participated in contests and won them, and bent their energies to go as far and accomplish as much as they could. "Of eighteen students," Scott reported, "seven made scores of 800 in the College Board examinations." Their work in high school had been speeded up, and the students had been through calculus by the time they took college boards. Scott spoke of the pleasure he took there in the precision and order of what he learned in mathematics. As he talked about the triangle, and what happens when you make a right angle, he made, with his hands, designs of geometrical figures. He liked the fact that you could set a problem and get the answer, that there was so much about his accomplishment that he could be certain of when he had done his work. He loved the manipulation of numbers, and took pleasure in speed and accuracy.

With the scholarship he would go to Harvard and be a mathematics student. Looking back three years later he described himself as coming with "some almost arbitrarily chosen leanings toward math," the subject in which he performed so well. He does not remember that he felt any "great passion for math, or for intellectual pursuits in general. . . . I came with a half-conscious faith in something I knew very little about."

The study of mathematics began auspiciously. He was placed in one of the courses organized for those bright advanced-placement high school students who were responding to the general effort to improve the quality of students' performance, and presumably his career as a mathematics student was launched:

> One thing freshman year did was to show me what math was. The excellent, rigorous approach by Professor Birkhoff in Math II

revealed math's logical underpinnings, and said that here was a field where I could find or develop this, this, and this knowledge or skill.

"But the Freshman Seminar Happened to Me"

THIS is the way Scott described the impact of the Freshman Seminar to which he was assigned, after choosing to be in one. (The seminars are described on pages 157–161.) David Riesman was in charge of one group of seminars, including the one Scott was assigned to, and all the seminars in that group dealt with issues and questions in the field of social relations. These students also registered for a Humanities course, and the two courses made up half of Scott's program. The other half was the mathematics course and one in French that he describes as "routine and review." In view of the excitement of the seminar it is probably just as well that he had one course that was routine and review.

The experience of the seminar was explosive. "I just hadn't thought about anything that was going on in the world." He had studied hard in high school, and "I accepted what people around me said as true"; and in the semirural community from which he came (although his was an academic family) many things were settled. "You know," he said, "it never occurred to me that everybody *didn't* like Ike — I was sure about him, too."

The most important thing about this seminar for Scott — and perhaps for others as well — was that students' questions about important issues were treated as serious questions. The faculty neither offered ready answers nor assumed that consideration of the questions students raised must wait for a later time. The purpose of the seminar, to encourage exploration of serious issues in terms important to students, was clear, and both teachers and students were free to make the exploration without the usual external instruments of organization. The absence of grades or ratings of any kind, examinations, and daily or even weekly required assignments made the intellectual inquiry itself the end to be sought. The seminar became for many of the students, and for Scott among them, an intellectual home. Three years later, students from the seminar, who had gone many different ways, still met to talk.

Writing of the seminar as a senior, Scott said he read more irregularly and wrote less than he should have that year. ". . . it was more a year of promise than accomplishment. One reason I wrote little was that I could see clearly that what I did write was poor indeed. The vast lack of knowledge on my part created false dilemmas and foolish writing."

But (he recalls) everything he had studied and everything he had done before the seminar seemed "boxed in" to him. One of the best things about that first year was that he was not, as he had been in high school, bound to study all subjects equally and at even pace. The "daily splintering of assignments" at school contrasted with the rhythm of the week at college:

> I could somehow work for several days at a single thing, a maneuver I liked very much.
>
> . . . .
>
> The year wasn't without depression, frustration, or rage. I recall the long February 22 week end as especially desperate; the "system" bore hard into me on occasion, as had never happened in high school. Ideas and emotions were widening within me; people and events were knocking down walls around me. . . . I like to think the whole thing left me uncertain (dogmatism dying) rather than puzzled. . . . I know myself better for having walked through the Yard. The idea of knowing yourself was foreign to me before Harvard.
>
> I am overwhelmed by Riesman's vision in creating the seminar, and am constantly struck (a Riesman phrase) by his comprehension of the modern situation. I am in no position to affirm or deny his analyses — this is not what I mean.

The year of promises either created or stirred up in Scott ideas that were to occupy him much of the time for the next two years, and his efforts to cope with them can be followed through the subjects he chose to study, the papers he wrote, the questions of personal belief and affiliation that dominated his thinking and his actions in the two years that followed, and out of which grew his later interest in politics and history:

> I remember liking Morris Cohen's autobiography, *A Dreamer's Journey,* a great deal. I read some Fromm and Maslow, and got it into my head that I ought to read more of them. Some of the stuff they gave us (e.g. David Smillie and Kurt Wolff) I couldn't make heads or tails of. . . . I discovered in my notes a projected bibliography for a paper I never started, which was to center around Ludwig von Bertalanffy's general system theory. I similarly almost started a paper on progress. One topic the seminar took up that was important to me was education. I took lots of notes from var-

ious places (John Dewey, Bertrand Russell, a book on Nazi education, some material on French education; and *The Place of Book-learning in Traditional Jewish Culture* by Mark Zborowski; the latter was my best-liked source on what kind of authority or lack thereof was right for educating a child well.

"What kind of authority or lack thereof" was a question that, in one form or another, occupied a lot of Scott's thought during the middle college years.

The problems the Freshman Seminar raised for Scott, or shaped out of interests hitherto undiscovered, were personal and self-centered problems. The question of personal freedom was constantly with him. He was troubled when he read about Jewish education because the discipline seemed harsh, but he had to conclude that the child was not damaged by the discipline, but "buoyed in his struggle" by the encouragement and interest of his relatives. "I had trouble thinking about this issue for a while, because I was an anarchist. I thought no one should ever be compelled to do anything." He read *The Vanishing Adolescent* by Edgar Friedenberg, Whyte's *Organization Man,* and Wylie's *Village in the Vaucluse.*

Along with his two roommates he became exercised by the events leading to the execution of Caryl Chessman in California. The two roommates were, he says, "stirred to terrific efforts. One, from Los Angeles, wrote to every Californian student he knew, urging them to appeal to Governor Brown, and to the California legislature, where an abolition of capital punishment bill was having a hard time." It was the circumstances of the execution that especially horrified Scott:

> There were *sixty* witnesses to it, and *thirty* of them were reporters. Chessman's post-execution letter to Will Stevens of the San Francisco Examiner strongly affected me. The best thing on capital punishment I've read since then has been Camus' "Reflections on the Guillotine."

The interest in capital punishment and in questions about crime that began here started him writing a paper on crime the next year which he finally finished in his junior year. Of that more later — but like most of what went on that first year, this was the starting point for thinking about problems of the relation of the individual to society — and that meant, in a large measure, at this point, problems of his own relation to society.

I have commented elsewhere (page 152) on the three kinds of

freshman year of the students I talked with — the repeat-performance year, the information-building year, and the shaking-up year. Some students had these experiences in combination, but freshman years are principally one or the other. Scott's was certainly a shaking-up period, and in the years that followed he was constantly involved in shaping the questions that the shaking up brought into his education, confronting them, and working at them.

An article called "In Praise of Academic Abandon" appeared in the Registration Issue of the *Harvard Crimson* in September 1961. The article described how important it was for some students to forget the demands of assignments and grades and read as though they were free men. Scott was beginning his sophomore year. He referred to that article in a letter he wrote later describing his second year and said "It struck me as a clear description of my relation to college, and I was delighted to learn that there were others like me around."

In his tutorial that second year he read Freud and wrote major papers: one on "Jim and Huck" for a course in American literature, and one on "Alienation and Alternatives" for the Social Relations course, and a third one for the tutorial based on his reading of Freud.

His writing that year, as the first year, was of two kinds — papers he chose to write because they helped him carry on his thinking about the subjects with which he was most involved, and papers he wrote to order. Of the latter he said some of the same harsh things he had said of such papers in the freshman year, but on reading them one finds that he has grown in his ability to deal objectively with a subject presented to him, and is better able to keep his eye on the object.

Of one of them, "Why Historians Disagree," he said it was "to some degree pedestrian, but I liked it." It was an analysis of two contemporary historians of France, and the assignment was to write on the subject indicated, in the light of Carl Becker's "Every Man His Own Historian." The topic was one of a long list of choices, and it is interesting that he chose it. It was his first analysis (and an intelligent one) of a subject in a field that was to become central to his thinking a year later. It was an historical consideration of issues in politics and social thought that, up to this point, had occupied him only in contemporary terms.

He reports with his usual candor:

> The paper I wrote on Stoicism and Christianity was hampered by the fact that I knew little about either philosophy. The paper was a last-minute effort before a deadline, and I didn't do nearly

enough reading for it. This made it poor as an examination of the two philosophies, but reflective of my own concerns, which I had to fall back on in order to write anything.

This is a fair sample of his general intellectual approach to whatever problem was at hand.

Conformity, Alienation, and Detachment

The detached person is conventionally adult no more, while the alienated person is not yet conventionally adult.

"CONFORMITY," "alienation" — these were the clichés of Scott's college generation — words that their elders used about them, and that they adopted. But his concern about conformity, and about how to become what he called a "lone man" without withdrawing from the world or rejecting it, but instead finding some way to function, was no attachment to a stereotype with Scott, nor were the words or ideas themselves clichés for him.

He had become sharply aware of his own need to cope with the world around him — how to define his relations to individual people, how much to conform to the conventions of the world he came from, how and in what ways to establish personal independence, how to act in a world grown physically, politically, ethically hazardous by reason of the atom bomb, the danger of war, political hostilities, and the problems of an economically affluent time. The questions that occupied him were intensely personal — he was speculating less about mankind than he was about himself. The reason for pointing this out is that the process of education in Scott's case shows, more clearly than the education of some students less single-minded than he was, the transition from this subjective, self-involved interest to a wider and more general concern with the same problems — a development that is one of the aims of liberal education.

He wrote a paper called "Alienation and Alternatives," which he referred to later as his "greatest effort to date. . . . It tied an awful lot of things together."

As in everything in his studies that had seriously captured his attention up to this time, his approach to the problem of alienation was almost exclusively individual. "The fundamental orientation of the paper is towards the individual. I am not equipped to deal with phenomena which are by definition group ones (e.g. public education). When I do speak in plurals, I am actually dealing in mere arithmetical multiplications of the individual situation."

He read a good deal: Daniel Bell's *Work and Its Discontents,* Erich Fromm, Paul Goodman, Maslow, Freud, and Sapir. He read the journals — the *Journal of Consulting Psychology,* the *Journal of Religion,* the *American Scholar,* and the *Journal of Sociology.* He read literary works — by Henry James, Nikos Kazantzakis, and Virginia Woolf. He read the angry young men, and writers who analyzed the angry young men.

He was hunting (as he was later when he was engrossed in questions about conscientious objection, pacifism, disarmament, and peace marches) for ways by which an individual might separate himself from those aspects of society — often the most basic ones — that he could not accept, and by the separation achieve a constructive life, not a withdrawn or hostile life. This paper, like others he wrote, and perhaps more than others, is an effort to use objective material as a means of dealing with matters in his own life about which he urgently needed to make choices.

Having read writers occupied with the concept of alienation, he turned for *his* definition of the term to a study of twenty Harvard students by Anthony Davids, who explored various "dispositions" of these students in 1955. Scott started as close to home as he could. He checked this definition with the writers whose work he read — psychoanalysts, sociologists, psychologists, and based his own discussion on the idea of the "lone man." He was trying to explore ways of being a "lone man" without being truly alienated from society:

> I think we may divide the lone man in society into two different types: the detached and the alienated. In general, alienation is a personal conflict, and detachment is not. This is because the detached individual has created not only his own path, but his own rewards. The alienated person, on the other hand, is never quite able to create personal satisfactions which compensate for the reinforcement he knows he could get by conforming.
>
> Alienation is pre-logical, half-realized, and frightening, while detachment is rather more under control of the individual. The detached person is aware of being detached, and is self-aware in general, more so than the alienated individual. The detached person is committed positively to certain goals and values.
>
> One of the features of alienation which I have observed is a tendency, seemingly psychopathic, to avoid adult reality. . . . No implication is here made that adult reality is real; the detached

person avoids it. However, the detached person is conventionally adult no more, while the alienated person is not yet conventionally adult. The former is not, like the latter, avoiding adult reality; he has faced it and grown past it. It is this avoidance, among other things, which explains why it is so uncomfortable to be alienated.

He identifies his "detached" person with Maslow's "self-actualizing" individual, but "I emphasize the detachment more than Maslow does." Self-actualizing people, he says, "are apart from society, and are almost precisely the opposite of alienated — they are autonomous, they have creative attitudes toward life."

He draws an imaginative parallel between Twain's *Huckleberry Finn* and Kerouac's *On the Road,* arguing in some detail that Huck Finn, unwilling to play the game of the society he knew, was a detached individual, and that Sal, also unwilling, was an alienated one. (More on this in "Literature in the Education of Scott Hansen," pages 31–39.)

The point of the paper is to examine not only the phenomenon of alienation itself, but ways detached men who cannot conform to society find of living creatively, as the alienated individual cannot. Of three ways, the first is the "courageous transformation of the running away into a running toward," which he finds in Kazantzakis's Odysseus, the modern man:

> who cannot settle down to comfortable virtues and betray the restless search. Traveling through the Western Mediterranean, Africa, and the Antarctic, Odysseus attempts to live so fully that eventual Death will have nothing to take from him. He always leaves havens without looking back, gradually accomplishing the "purification his vision of God must undergo, from the pure beast to the pure spirit."

The second alternative is artistic creativity:

> Artistic creativity arises out of contact with the unconscious part of the mind, and results in the emergence of original and individual products. This ability to articulate, in any of various ways, from deep within one's self distinguishes the artist. It may be argued that the artist is necessarily a lone man, alienated from others; his creativity is, I think, his saving grace.

Scott thought of artistic creativity and direct courageous struggling as "attempts to do something *with* alienation"; and describes what he thinks must be done *about* alienation.

His third approach is to examine love as an attempt to do something about alienation. "I am skating on relatively thin ice, for my comments depend on the choice of a particular definition of love." He read Freud's *On Creativity and the Unconscious,* and rejected the definition of love as "aim-inhibited sexuality."

> For Maslow, the case was entirely different. One of the most important characteristics of his self-actualizing people was their ability to resolve seemingly basic dichotomies (particularly the masculine-feminine one). I tend toward Maslow's view of love, and Fromm's, which is essentially similar.

. . . .

> Freud, it may be said, held human nature to be split between sex and aggression, between the life- and death-instincts. It is a not unreasonable paraphrase of Fromm to say that he would see aggression as the first thing that occurs to the individual upon realization of his essential aloneness; he would add that this is not a fully human action, and that one ought rather to build up patiently "to love as the answer to human existence." Maslow would have it that human needs are "good or neutral rather than evil." Now, even in the face of an assertion that, say, love was peripheral at best, I should insist that the world situation is such that the cultivation of love is highly desirable, perhaps necessary.

As he develops the argument of his paper, Scott moves from consideration of the individual personality to consideration of how this approach to life (which he wishes to offer as an alternative to alienation) involves the society in which the individual lives. "The question of who ultimately to blame, society or the individual, for widespread alienation and lack of commitment is difficult."

As he reaches the end of his argument and his paper, Scott makes the connection between his thoughts about how the single individual may escape alienation, and the moral and political considerations that are to occupy a good deal of his attention for the next year. In an interview near the middle of his junior year it was clear that his attention at that point, coupled with a good deal of anxiety, was turned to such matters as conscientious objection, disarmament, and pacifism.

Toward the close of this paper he quotes the following passage which he found, he says, "deep in the back of the *Handbook for Conscientious Objectors":*

> Love is a hard word to say in the smoking-room atmosphere of the draft board, the board members may be embarrassed and a little peevish to hear it mentioned. It is fitting, however, that the objector be bold in the knowledge that he (however unworthy) is with the prophets, and that his inquisitors (however worthy) are

speaking for the dead past out of which man is creeping. It is not right that the advocates of love should apologize or flinch.

There is a religious cast to his thinking at this point. There is other evidence of religious interest in that sophomore year, in the course of which he participated in an extracurricular seminar at Phillips Brooks House on "Theology in the Theatre." This quality was questioned by his tutor in a conversation at the end of that year. More than a year later Scott commented on this criticism:

> The tutor thought the paper on alienation was too beautiful, too religious. He thought I was too mystical, not realistic, that I dealt in symbols rather than explanations. He advised that I read some Hemingway or Dostoyevski. I don't know how much this lecture affected me. I resented it so much that I put away the notes I'd scribbled during it and completely forgot about it. On the other hand, I have very definitely moved in the directions he advised then. This may be due merely to the passage of time.

"Junior Year Everything Fell Apart"

Scott recalled that "Junior year everything fell apart." He said this at the beginning of his senior year, when he was already on the road toward putting together what, a year before, had fallen apart. It had been obvious in January of his junior year, in a long interview, that his work, his life at college, and his feelings were dislocated. He was fighting the dean — he wanted to get out of the dormitory and live by himself, and he was not permitted to do it. The reasons he had were not good enough. "They make it more intolerable by forcing you to stay in"; and he wrote a letter to the dean enlightening him on the subject. He was fighting his work, too. "I've been cutting classes — I just don't go." He thought it a poor idea, he said, but he somehow couldn't make himself go. He spoke with a kind of wry humor about the fact that Harvard forced you to live in the dormitory, but made no objection to your cutting classes.

He was trying to write a paper on crime. The thesis seemed to be that neither the idea that criminals were evil and must be punished, nor the contemporary view that they should be viewed as psychologically sick, was necessarily correct. "Sometimes they have a very high degree of skill, are simply living in different terms from the rest of society"; and he spoke of the skill and sharpness and intelligence it takes to be a good criminal. The best ones, he said, don't get caught — just as the sharpest people living inside the social system don't get caught at doing wrong things they do:

> The gulf between the criminal and non-criminal is not so much psychological as sociological. I see much more relevance for crime in the middle and lower class structures in America than in the psychological structures of health and sickness.
>
> .   .   .   .
>
> The seeds of crime lie not in disorganization, but in the apperceived or actual disparity between peoples which arises out of social stratification.

The argument and illustrations in the paper are directed mainly toward discussion of the disparity between middle-class values and lower-class values, and the consequent repressive behavior, through law and custom, of the middle class toward the lower class.

At the time of the first interview that junior year he had not been able to finish the paper, but he thought he would make another try at it. The subject came up six months later — had the paper ever been finished?

> Oh yes, I finished it. It wasn't much good. It was a confused kind of paper. I think I was getting all my resentments into it — all my resentments against the middle class, that means my mother; so it wasn't entirely objective. It wasn't one of my better papers, no.

Then he added:

> I'm doing a paper on Hoover now; it's much better. . . . I'm generally doing better; I'm going to all my classes now.

In the middle of his fighting, during the first part of that junior year — fighting the dormitory, the dean who wouldn't let him move out, the classes he wouldn't go to, and the paper he couldn't finish — he thought, as students so often do in these circumstances, about dropping out of college for a year.

A number of the students I talked with had considered leaving college, even though in many cases they were doing quite acceptable work. Several of them had actually taken such a moratorium year with varying degrees of success (see pages 146, 148). Although there are many individual reasons for the success or failure of the year away, there are some common elements. The students whose imaginations are captured by something outside the college — something they might do if they were not in college — often have successful leave-of-absence years. Stephen Hertz discovered in a year out of college that he could not bring to the study of sculpture what was needed to become a good sculptor ("I learned the difference between being an amateur and being a professional"); but he could bring to the study of medicine what was needed to become a good doctor. He needed to find that out, and a year out of college settled the matter. He returned to go on with his pre-medical studies. Others, who fly from college with no place to fly *to,* who (unlike Stephen) move away from something, but have nothing in mind to move *toward,* often find that mere freedom from college is not what they needed. Some of them have very frustrating years. It was this that Scott feared: "The trouble is," he said, "I think I'd just deteriorate, and not do anything with the year." He had nothing in mind when he thought of leaving, except to escape; and he decided against that.

He considered what would happen if he left college — and in the front of his mind was the fact that he would probably be called into the army. He said he thought he really was a conscientious objector, but, he added "I don't think I could claim exemption on those grounds if what I really wanted was to be out of school." The feelings are mixed here, as in all the other aspects of his personal and academic life.

During the early part of this junior year Scott was lashing out at his surroundings, but he was beginning to think about some of the moral and political implications of the same ideas that had occupied him the year before on a more personal basis. The papers on alienation, on the nature of the "lone man" who might be destructively "alienated" but might be constructively "detached," on Huck Finn's ability to grow up and Sal's inability to grow up, led beyond the personal concerns they express into an effort to clear up some ideas about how to deal with urgent current issues — disarmament and war. They led him to decide that the study of Freud and Maslow and Fromm, the reading of literature, was not enough to give him direction — that he must also study history and politics.

The problem of whether or not to take the stand of the conscientious objector was in the middle of the confusions of the first part of the junior year, and he spent a lot of energy in arguments about disarmament. He joined *Tocsin,* and gave a great deal of time and energy to its activities; he participated in the Washington Peace March; and as he began to resolve, at least temporarily, some of the questions that had been troubling him, things became less chaotic, his work went better, and he began to find it absorbing.

When he was considering leaving college and declaring himself a conscientious objector, he talked about the danger of taking drastic action that might be only a "symbolic act" and might at the same time close off opportunity for constructive action. For him, as for others, the Washington Peace March was a symbolic act that did not cut off the opportunity for continuing action. It served an important function for him, as a declaration:

> We went down in buses, overnight. It was rather uncomfortable but we can take it. We picketed the White House the first day, but it was the next day that really counted — there were thousands and thousands of people. We were well policed, and there was no disorder. It probably doesn't make much sense, but it felt good. And we talked with Congressmen. I talked with a very conservative Congressman from my district. That was a fruitless thing to do, but there was a tremendous spirit generated at least among our people there. And then we made a silent march to the cemetery — that tremendous crowd of people. I had read about how the British do that — march silently from one place to another. There was nothing garish about it. Somebody said "be quiet" and we were, and you could just hear the sound of footsteps going through the cemetery, and back down. . . . I'm sure that sort of thing can't be done again and again. It would get full of professional demonstrators, and that isn't what this was. As a one-shot thing it was wonderful — all those people. It let you see that there were other people around.

During these months he decided the position of the conscientious objector was not a tenable one, for him, and during the spring vacation in his home town he spoke on pacifism at a supper forum of his home church:

> For some time now, I have been much concerned with questions of peace and war in our time, and particularly with pacifism as one response to these questions.
>
> .   .   .   .
>
> My personal decision, after long consideration, has been against conscientious objection. An act of conscience like this is not, to my mind, a sufficient end in itself. The overriding consideration is not consistency, unswerving adherence to principle, but the effectiveness of one's actions in bringing about ends desired. In Christian terms, I seek not to avoid evil but to counter it, which may involve me in other evils. Evil is not necessarily best coped with by

dramatic one-shot stands like C.O. A quieter, more difficult, and more significant way of demonstrating where your moral intent lies is to have the long-run meaning of your life speak for the principles involved.

Even as I have drawn away from C.O. as a method, I have drawn closer to feeling the importance of the aims of pacifism. Participation in a war is a very difficult thing to accept or at least it ought to be. Though one must accept the fact of evil in the world, and in particular the inescapable presence of evil in oneself, I don't think we need accept as inevitable one of society's greatest evils, war. War is not a spontaneous offshoot of man's sinfulness, but a highly organized, and even artificially created, type of conflict.

"Things Are Better Now"

WHEN we began to talk after a five-month interval, at the end of that junior year, "Things are better now," was Scott's first remark. "What's better?" "Oh, everything. For one thing, spring is here, and things get better in spring." In the interval he had thought a lot, felt a lot, acted a lot, and worked. There was a new girl — "she's very important in what I do." The kind of companionship he had felt as a freshman in the seminar he felt again with the people involved in the new steps he was taking, as when he went on the Washington Peace March and joined *Tocsin:*

> You know, when you get off alone things can look very bad, you think about them and distort them. For instance, I was so much involved in disarmament, and thought so much about it, making all sorts of rationalizations.

His work was going better, he said. He was not cutting classes. He spoke especially of a biology course, where they had been studying genetics. Part of his interest came out when he mentioned the work they were doing on hormones: "That's my father's field — he's in plant science. It's interesting to sit there and hear them describe things I've heard my father talk of for a long time." And then he spoke of a "geneticist who is one of the great men in the field, who's written the standard text in the field — he's in my father's department."

What he spoke most about, though, was a psychology course in which they were studying motivation. The subject appears to have relevance to many of the matters he had struggled with since his freshman year, but the course itself "represented an unpleasant inroad on my time and effort." He wanted to get at an understanding of motivation, but his feelings about the course were mixed:

> It's a graduate school type of course — you just have to get all the information you can. The main work for the student is working on a special paper — a subject like Curiosity — and you're expected to do an actual experiment — the sort of thing that appears in the Journals. The main thing is the volume of information you get. It's like a chess game. You get the subject's response to all sorts of questions and you try to put together all the facts and information you gather, and try to fit them together in terms of one theory or another of motivation. You put them together and try to see where there are contradictions and then you look at everything you have. That's how it's like a chess game — you look at it all and then you move. . . .
>
> It does have to do with the motivation of people, but it's presented in such a mechanical way, and you rate everything — it's presented in a listing kind of way; there are three major points and everything has to fit into that.

Asked why he thought about majoring in psychology if he felt this way about the kind of study he was engaged in, he said:

> Well, my real interests came out in the seminars, in sociology and anthropology; but I've needed the basic courses in psychology. I know something about it now. The most important part of it has come out in the papers I've written — they are what has mattered most. I feel I can be competent in psychology. I can write a good exam; I can pull out what I need to know from the reading I've done. No, I'm not really in it reluctantly. Sometimes I think I can use what I've been learning here in connection with the kind of interest I have in *Tocsin* — disarmament; that's really a permanent, abiding interest, and I think I'll just go on the way I am, with that.

Asked if anything he studied was as important to him as the question of disarmament, there was a very long pause. . . :

> Well, I'm always trying to find out something about it, so I can understand more. I'm always looking for a good book — I'm looking now for a really good book on Russia, and a good book on economics to read this summer. It all belongs together; I'm trying to fit it together into a world view — well, not a world view, but a position, yes, a position so I can think about it. This *Tocsin* is all student-run and there aren't many people to go to, to ask about this.
>
> But this is off the track of the question. I think the same way about the paper I'm writing on Curiosity — that's an assignment, but once I've settled on the topic I like to go all round that, too,

they're not one different from the other. It's just that you have a whole lot of wants there, you have a whole series of interests that you balance.

Scott was obviously not clear yet about where he was headed, or what the next steps would be; but there was a difference in his manner, and his views about himself and his work were different from the attitudes he had had five months before:

Things aren't solved, but they don't overwhelm me. I go two or three days at a time, and I just keep moving — not frantically, but just going. . . . I've settled down. I know what my interests are. I don't get too upset; I don't feel hurt, I can work. Before, so many things seemed possible, seemed open to me, and I was confused, and I didn't know what to think. I used to think of all sorts of things I might do. But now there are two or three things that interest me and I can work at them, and I am sure these will last for say ten years at least, and I'm sure there will be other developments to keep going with after that.

About the work, I don't actually know. I haven't handed anything in, to get grades on or anything, but I have a pretty good idea — some idea but not altogether. Grades help — they let me know whether I'm just cockeyed, going down a road, speaking my own private language. The work is going better — it's just going, now. It used to be just blah. I remember, I particularly remember the billiard tables at the house. I used to get all tense trying to read, and I'd go down there to escape and I'd just shoot, I remember. I'd say to myself, "I'll go down there and relax and then come back and hit the books again." I'd go there and have to wait for the table — there's only one table — and I'd sit there maybe half an hour waiting, and I wouldn't relax at all, it was ridiculous. But that doesn't happen now.

He was now ending his junior year and at this moment of his education and his thought about himself and how he was functioning there were apparently three points of attention — three points from which he moved. One was the strong feeling for the ideas *Tocsin* represented for him, feelings which the Washington Peace March satisfied — "it let you see that there were other people around"; the second was the character of his interest in his work; the third was a not-yet-articulate need to make some kind of coherent design for action out of these interests.

Scott resisted the teaching of his tutor that term as he did the approach of the psychologist with whom he studied:

He draws diagrams on the board, he makes analogies, he puts ideas into boxes, he reduces complex things to simple things . . .

it's an approach — it's like what Maslow says, this pedestrian approach to scholarship, where you try to fit things quickly into pigeonholes — it's a rejection of the fact that when you're working things out it's going to be indeterminate, it's going to be up in the air and you just have to put up with the uncertainty for a while till you work things out — it's a rejection of thinking, it's an assumption that mechanistically things will just come, you can just plug them in and chug along.

About the general state of his work he said:

.   .   .   .

About my work — *Tocsin* is a kind of general overriding impassioned interest. In work there isn't that way-up-there overriding interest, but I like to puzzle over what the nature of curiosity is. The material is interesting, and then when you feel you have understood something, that's a good thing. . . . Take a paper for another course, now at eleven tomorrow the lecture begins. Now I'll go home tonight, and I've got some ideas, and I'll revolve them around and go to bed. It's like being in a room with a whole bunch of wheels turning — it's like the television act, the guy who spins plates on the ends of sticks and he spins one and then goes over and spins another, and keeps them all going. That's the way it is with work — if you keep all the things spinning, you're okay — you won't, though; there is another cycle, and you get panicked again, but at least you get to know you can get out of it. Oh, I hope I can get out of it. There's the business of time — it's so short; but if I can just keep going they sort of come.

A lot of time is spent attending lectures. A lot comes through if you are paying attention to a lecture. I'm not keeping up entirely with my reading; I've never been able to do it all, but I'm covering the material in the courses as well as I ever have. . . . Sometimes I don't do anything with *Tocsin* at all. I just work all week in the library.

But these things aren't so different, he pointed out, and he spoke of the boy who wanted to write a piece about the Berlin Wall for their *Tocsin* sheet, and sat in the library basement reading all the issues of *The New York Times* from May to September — "fanatic, you may call it." He spoke of the Committee of Correspondence and the interest of faculty members — Riesman, and others* — in the matters that were occupying him and his friends:

The peace movement desperately needs intellectuals, not because it is a vested interest with them, but because it needs people

* Including Stuart Hughes, who was later to run for the Senate on a similar platform.

who can actually work things out, can work at the economics of disarmament. . . . Some students at MIT are pushing for a peace research institution, and they think MIT can set it up because as universities go they have money.

But that's not all of college life, you know. I just got my bicycle out of hock, where it's been all winter. I was so glad to have it, I rode around about two hours. The weather is nice, spring. It's too bad everything is so busy . . . well, it's not coasting, anyhow, it's just a sense of functioning with some kind of shape to things — for now at least.

The most important reading and writing Scott did that junior year was for a paper that registered both the end of his uneasy thrashing around, and his developing interest in the general meaning, in history and contemporary life, of some of the ideas which had become important the first year, and had stayed with him throughout. The paper was on Herbert Hoover, and its thesis was that Hoover's failure as a President was owing to his inability to escape the imprisonment of his own ideology. In areas in which Hoover's image of American individualism was not threatened, or not at issue, he performed with distinction, and Scott's paper is a detailed analysis of the kind of situation in which he could function constructively, and the kind in which he could not. Reading Hoover's state papers and other writings leads Scott to describe the failure that follows refusal to deal with issues that demand understanding and action not measured by the terms of a rigid definition:

One of the most significant aspects [of this ideology of American individualism] is what might be called false generalization. Hoover projected his own views onto the world and spoke of them as general truth. For instance, he often indicated in his speeches that the New Deal was destroying American traditions, when it was merely rejecting him. Hoover's lack of detailed information in American history caused him to think that practically all agitation for a different political system from the one he favored was imported from Europe. Hoover also projected onto his arch-opponent, FDR. He often stated that FDR was trying to impose a new system on the American people. Indeed, changes were being made, but there was little evidence that a new system (Hoover meant ideology) was being created or that the people were being imposed upon.

American individualism was, like all ideologies, an idea system believed in such a way that it could continue to be maintained under severe strain. Many ideologies (e.g. that of Robert Welch) could not stand up under the least bit of reality testing. It is striking that Hoover could be so sure he was right that he would stake more on a comparatively unlikely future evil — the loss of America's self-reliance, etc. — than on a comparatively certain present evil — a dispirited and suffering nation. This is one of ideology's great strengths and weaknesses. The adherence to an ideal which sometimes loses track of reality.

Another significant feature of Hoover's mind is that his ideology governs only a well-marked-off area of it. He seems to think ideologically solely in the area of politics; moreover within his political philosophy, Hoover's ideology covers domestic policy only, and economic policy in the main. This delineation of limits around the province of American individualism in Hoover's mind bedevils attempts to explain the origins of it. If the fact of Hoover's thinking ideologically were due to some general variable like limited intelligence, why should the blind spot exist in but one part of his outlook?

It is not a significant point against Hoover that he approved of policies later shown to be disastrous; he was but sharing the common tendency to see one's own good luck as just, natural, and permanent. The Depression, however, is another story. Though we cannot criticize the exaltation of merely apparent economic health, we can criticize the denial of highly conspicuous economic failure. This is what Hoover engaged in during the Thirties. And he did so because of his ideology of American individualism.

What is important in Scott's history is that this paper, and the ideas that prompted it, marked the end of his preoccupation with the purely individual plight or the purely individual possibilities, and his recognition that he could not pursue the questions that absorbed him without knowing more about history and politics.

"Political Concern Became the Theme"

THE next conversation with Scott took place over a cup of coffee in a coffee shop in Harvard Square, in October of his senior year. He handed me almost at once a letter he had written to the Committee on Undergraduate Instruction earlier that month petitioning for a change in his senior thesis topic. Early the spring before he had expected to write on Freud. "Now I would like to write a thesis in Political Science." He explained the reasons for his change of topic:

Sophomore year I became a Social Relations major for various reasons, one of them a strong interest in psychoanalysis. In sophomore Tutorial I developed some ideas about part of Freud's thought. However, my concerns have been changing. Last year in Social Relations 98 I wrote papers on the sociology of crime and Herbert Hoover as President, first and second terms respectively. My reading this summer has been in politics and history. These topics, and especially political ethics, are insistently calling for attention in my mind.

He submitted, along with this letter, the required statement about his thesis topic:

Several personal intellectual themes have converged to give rise to my thesis topic, which will be in the history of political thought. I'm very interested in the history of Europe between the two World Wars, particularly the second of these two decades. Europe then was a disintegrating society; outstanding aspects of the breakdown were the depression and totalitarianism. At the time, men actively sought for answers to these difficulties both on the right and on the left. Many have studied the political right of the Thirties; I should like to study the left.

A continuing problem for the leftist, one which was aggravated by the events of the 1930's, is how far left to be. Most every thinking person holds values radically to the left of contemporary realities, and is faced with the question of how radical an advocacy to maintain. An example from our chosen context is the belief Orwell expressed in 1936, that socialism was the only possible effective enemy of fascism. Since it actually turned out to be a Tory, not a socialist, Great Britain that waged war so well against the Axis, we may presume that believing as Orwell did could engender a good deal of wasted political effort. I would like to know more about this kind of error of judgment. I am inclined to think that socialism was a good ultimate answer to the problems of the Thirties, but I wonder very hard whether a socialist stand was the best one to take in the circumstances. The question of judgment is constant here. Not only the desirable, but the possible too, must enter into one's political stands.

For reasons that need not be detailed, I've chosen the intellectual left of Great Britain as my object of study in the inter-war period. My central concern is not the judgments that have been made at a later time upon the Thirties, but history as it unfolded. I want to know about the writers of the times, who did not know what was going to happen, rather than later writers, who had hindsight. There are a number of specific foci possible within the English left. An obvious one is the Fabian Society. Anne Freemantle has termed the Thirties and the Second World War a period of "anxious and attentive reappraisal" for the Fabians. One way to get at this reappraisal would be to read the *New Statesman,* which commented on political developments week by week throughout these years. However, even the best journalism may be too immediate for our purposes. I could delve into the publications of the Left Book Club, though it was not begun until 1936. Still another alternative is to study the thought of one man. I find George Orwell a compelling writer and would really enjoy dealing with him.

I'm not sure how much specialism is demanded in a thesis. If I studied a broad group of people, I might want to pick out one issue or theme for study. The classic one, and it is still fascinating, is the growing disillusionment with Communism and the great Russian experiment. Another interesting theme is the pacifism of the British left. It is striking that this response to war should be sought the more even as militarism came to the fore on the Continent. A precise choice of topic does not have to be made immediately. Presently, I'm doing general reading to gain a firm idea of what the Thirties were.

After the October conversation he wrote a long letter about his thinking at the time:

My political concern had for a long time been sporadic and extracurricular. I read about the Freedom Rides, sit-ins and the like with interest; I was very interested in a student magazine that originated in Swarthmore, called *Albatross.* Somewhere along that winter, I had joined *Tocsin,* a very intelligent disarmament group. The first appearance of the political angle in my required work was the spring tutorial paper, on Hoover. Compare it to the fall term one on crime. I can see every difference in the world. Mainly, the emotional content permeating the crime paper has been drained from the latter one. It wasn't that I wasn't working on something personally important; rather, I'd shoved my personal conflicts enough to the side that I was concentrating on the objective situation, on Hoover and FDR as Presidents.

There's a lot less reading that I can point to as important in this political gambit than in earlier ones. The subject matter is not approached so much through inspirational literature, as through mere accumulation of facts. For instance, one important book has been Richard Barnet's *Who Wants Disarmament?;* it's not an inspiration like François Villon, but a comprehensive history of the disarmament negotiations. Sometimes I feel that I've read so many books that I couldn't be swept off my feet by any single book again. Charles Osgood's essay in *The Liberal Papers* and the 23rd chapter ("A Pagan Sermon") of Mills' *The Causes of World War Three* are short pieces that have impressed me a good deal. Koestler's *Darkness at Noon* was educational, and I especially learned from Robert Penn Warren's *All the King's Men.* My thesis work ought to be a major step toward a political awareness, but presently I am chipping *very* slowly at such key questions as why Americans are so obsessed with Communism.

This year is still all plans and no results, but I have been very actively building the necessary foundations for the next six months. In wildest general terms, my task of the next few years is to gain an understanding of history and politics, and come to some tenets of a political philosophy. Gaetano Salvemini (an Italian historian about whom I know nothing) has said: "We cannot be impartial. We can only be intellectually honest ... aware of our passions and on guard against them. Impartiality is a dream, and honesty a duty." Right now I want *competence* badly. For what? Who can be sure? I want to play a part in the creation of a responsible political left in the United States. We need intelligent activists, not merely activists. The U.S. has too many Micawbers, people waiting for something to turn up. It's easy to make radical criticisms of certain aspects of our current situation. Some of our foreign policy, like our China policy, is practically bankrupt. Domestically, people are busily refusing to face automation left and right. While I speak radically, I recognize that I am young. I'm not speaking here of a sociological commonplace that leftist youths move to the right as they age. I'm referring to the meeting of the good and the possible, ends and means if you will, that is politics. The conscientious objection stand I nearly took was a purely moral one. Now, as I gather in facts, I'm working my way back toward the possible.

That year Scott Hansen finished his undergraduate life. It was not a distinguished career by most observable academic standards. Even this final year, when he had moved out of the self-preoccupation of the earlier time and had reached some convictions, temporary ones, at least, about how he should function in society, he did not perform consistently on the good academic level his intelligence warranted and the college would like. He learned a good deal and he was always engaged in working at problems that were important to him — and indeed were important ones for a young man in this time to be concerned with. He had no eye for the practical advantages to be gained by keeping his attention on his scholastic record. He was absorbed in what he was studying and thinking about:

> In my four courses last fall [he wrote in the middle of his final semester] I got an A and a B in the two that interested me least — the A in a statistic course that was very easy for me (I had to take some Social Relations methods course or other); the B in an extremely sloppily organized child psychology course, for which nevertheless I wrote a good paper.

Of a history course in which he got a C+ he said:

> It was a course on American political traditions . . . it's the same
> thing this spring in a government course in the nation's party pol-
> itics . . . I'm working fairly hard in it, as I did in the history course,
> but still I bump along with C grades. I suspect the problem is that
> I just don't know enough yet . . . I can't distinguish good sources
> from bad . . . I suspect that mere passage of time, and saturation
> with a subject matter makes one smarter in the subject, and I
> simply haven't learned enough government or history yet. My last
> course (besides the thesis) is Louis Hartz on classical liberal
> democracy and its critics. . . . This is a fine course; Hartz is a fine
> man, and is talking about things I want to know about. Hartz is
> concerned with whether classical liberalism has or can survive
> various intellectual and historical attacks on it, such as Freud and
> Marx. He thinks that it has (in a much more cautious form). I
> suspect that this is so in America, but not in Britain, where some-
> thing better has replaced it.

Scott's ideas about what he would like to do for his senior thesis
had taken shape. What he ended up with was a study of the non-Com-
munist intellectuals who left Britain to fight in the Spanish Civil War. In
explaining his choice of this subject he said:

> My political stance is somewhat to the left, and that is one rea-
> son I have studied the left. So many people have dissected the right
> that we must even up the score. I am very interested in the place of
> a political left in a nation: What kinds of policies will it offer? Will
> they be effective? A particular concern is the intellectual as leftist,
> as politician.
> But make no mistake. I have not merely been working out my
> own problems in a disguised form. Once a study begins it gains a
> momentum of its own. First I thought of the Spanish war as a glo-
> rious cause: I, too, wanted to pay homage to Catalonia. But the
> more I found out about the Britain these men had come from, the
> less noble their leaving it looked. So then the question of *why* they
> left attained a new importance. And way led on to way . . . and the
> results follow.

This he wrote as what he calls the "personal preface" to his paper.

His principal thesis is that, after MacDonald's "betrayal" of the
Labour Party in 1931, the deep disenchantment of the intellectuals with
the possibilities for achieving their purposes in Britain sent them off to
fight the Spanish cause.

> The widespread sympathy for the Spanish Republic which came
> into being so remarkably fast after Franco revolted stemmed more

from discontent with conditions in Britain than knowledge of conditions inside Spain.

> The Spanish Civil War is an extraordinary event, because in addition to being an historic phenomenon by conventional standards, it was also an intellectual event of great importance.

He contrasts the response to the Spanish war with the response to the Russian revolution on the part of left intellectuals. He speaks of the great importance of the Russian revolution to such men, but quotes a comment that "even in the best years the outside sympathy for Soviet Russia was political and cerebral. . . . The Soviet System elicited intellectual approval, the Spanish struggle aroused emotional identification" and he speaks of the Spanish war as "probably the zenith of political idealism in the first half of the 20th century."

After discussing the spirit with which the intellectuals he studied went to Spain, Scott wrote three short "case histories" of men who especially interested him — George Orwell, Julian Bell, and Geoffrey Garratt:

> Orwell went to the war utterly alone and remained so during and after it. Garratt is the least radically left of those Britons who permitted the war to mean a great deal to them. . . . Bell was one of the most exciting and creative Britons who went off to war.

In the end, in spite of deep admiration for some — not all — of the intellectuals who found in the war a cause with which to identify, he concludes — and this conclusion, reasonable or not, is the place at which his own education arrived by the time it came formally to a close — that in most cases there was not much "material reason" for a British left thinker to get excited about Spain:

> Such men had Labour policy problems to think about, and also the task of rebuilding a Labour Party which was shaken by the MacDonald betrayal. The response to Spain demonstrated a sharp alienation from Britain on the part of these respondents. This showed when they got to Spain — in much of the writing is the assertion that they and the Republic are alone against the world.
>
> The Spanish war was a clear and dramatic sphere of acting, which gave them a way of dealing with their frustration, uncertainty and alienation.

He quotes Mannheim's view that groups of low status who are trying to gain more status are likely to evidence the utopian mentality, likely to be driven into complete opposition to the prevailing order by their failure to gain ascendancy within it:

> Intellectuals are not a group driven into opposition to the pre-
> vailing order by failure to gain ascendancy within it. It was rather
> their *own* failure to *use* the ascendancy they possessed that led to
> their frustration and consequent readiness to respond to the Span-
> ish Civil War. By emphasizing the "betrayal" of MacDonald's co-
> alition to the right in 1931 these men were in effect externalizing a
> failure that was actually partly their own, the utter lack of adequate
> policy during the second Labour government which brought Mac-
> Donald into a position to act as he did.

And finally:

> It is striking to note that in spite of the obvious fact that in this
> world one never achieves more than intermediate status, many of
> those who went to Spain saw the Loyalist cause as an end state,
> quite literally as heaven on earth.

Scott's paper created dissension among the men who read it and judged it; and his oral "defense" created even more. His tutor thought well of the paper; a distinguished sociologist who had read the paper and commented on it at length thought well of it. An historian objected because Scott did not go farther back in history for the background of his discussion of the political situation in Britain which caused this group of men to turn their backs on Britain and go to Spain; a sociolo-gist objected because Scott did not have the demographic data that would give an adequate picture of the range of people who went from Britain to Spain to fight. He used terms loosely — "pragmatism" and "objective reality"; and his examiners wanted definitions. The paper was "larded and loaded . . . with value judgments [made] unashamedly and without effort to conceal his subjectivity."

Probably all the scholarly objections to Scott's paper were valid, and it was suggested that perhaps he should have been warned that the paper would be judged largely on these grounds, "although warning would have made no difference to Scott Hansen who is very much his own man." His tutor pointed out that he had gone carefully into the evidence about the attitudes and actions of the intellectuals who inter-ested him, and he "learned from the work he did on the thesis to take a different attitude to British volunteering in the Spanish Civil War than that with which he began." The examiner, more favorable toward his work than others, described the defense of his thesis as knowledgeable, articulate and forceful, despite nervousness, although neither graceful nor resilient.

For our purposes the main thing to be said about Scott Hansen's final study at Harvard is what it tells us about the line of search that began with astonishment at the complexities of a world he had scarcely looked at when he entered Harvard, that was self-involved and self-exploring for several years until it turned to question his own values and his possible place in a world of action. His last effort in his Harvard education was an effort to find out how other men, more talented than he, a little older, had at an earlier dramatic moment in contemporary history followed the search in their terms.

He ended his college career without distinction or acclaim. At almost no time in the course of it, except at the disintegrated period of the junior year, which also he grew out of, did he stop trying to discover what he should think and do, and how he might find out.

Postscript, March, 1964

LETTERS happened to arrive from all four of the students whose stories are in this book, just as the work was going to press. Scott Hansen's letter indicates that he did not find his struggles at an end when he finished Harvard. He is in a good graduate school, and had a hard time the first semester. This letter, though, says, "Things are looking up a lot — there are a number of wonderful professors, and I am on my way."

II

Literature in the Education of Scott Hansen

SCOTT HANSEN in describing his work spoke often of his reading of literature, but he never turned his attention to literature as an academic subject. He took only one conventional English course during his four years at Harvard — a course in American Literature. Although he both talked and wrote a good deal about his interests — indeed his attention was most often focused on an effort to understand what his interests were, why he had them, and where they might lead him — there is little to show that he was "interested in literature." He paid attention neither to literary history nor to systems of criticism. And there is a remarkable difference in the quality of the papers he wrote, and indeed in the way he talked about literature when he was filling an assignment requiring him to write about a literary work, and when he was drawing upon his reading of literature for illumination of issues, questions, and ideas with which he was primarily occupied. That is, from the point of view of a literary critic, his relation to literature was limited.

Any teacher of literature has periods of doubt about just what "English papers" accomplish for the intellectual life of a student, and although the writing of such papers is no more academic or formalistic than the writing of papers in other disciplines, many of us have an uneasy feeling that in the process of writing such papers students often lose the life and meaning of the literary experience. One cannot read papers on literary subjects of the sort produced by students in English courses without realizing how often a student fails to come anywhere near the heart of a literary work, fails to take in the complex quality of its art. One realizes also that often he has been engaging in a kind of literary exposition required of him, which has no connection with the meaning of the literary work to him.

Scott wrote papers based on his reading of literature in several courses, especially in those in the Humanities, and naturally in the American Literature course. The Humanities course of his freshman year was, along with the Seminar, the occasion of his departure from mathematics, of his start in a new direction in pursuit of his education. He referred in his senior year to the literary content of this freshman course, in which he "gained an appreciation that is still with me for several individual authors, such as Gerard Manley Hopkins." But the sixteen "exercises," on literature, history, etc., that were the required writing for this course, were for him indeed "exercises." Three years later, speaking of a paper on *The Faerie Queene,* he wrote:

> The assignments were detailed and the papers hard. I enclose a typical assignment and paper. I got a B on it, but believe me I did not understand Spenser at all. There were 16 of these short papers in the course. On almost all of them, I understood only half of what they were after. I did well or poorly by chance. I stabbed in the dark, sometimes succeeding, sometimes not. . . . By the end of the year I had gotten the knack of writing the papers and enjoyed doing the last one on Frost.

In the paper he carefully followed the assignment to "write an essay about the attitude (or attitudes) toward human love" to be found in particular stanzas of a particular canto of the poem. Several specific questions were asked, and students were to include answers to these questions in the essay. "Note that you are not simply to describe types of love in general terms, but to derive your conclusions from particular uses of language."

Scott followed these instructions and his brief paper abounds in specific reference to metaphors Spenser uses for aspects of love and, in fact, shows in concrete ways a capacity for rather subtle observation. He may have learned more than he thinks from the need to observe such details, and the demand that he turn his mind to specific questions; but he was, and remained through the year, impatient with this method, although certain that the course itself was important to his growth.

But in other ways literature was of immense importance to him and he made lavish use of it in his later thinking about ethics, politics, psychology, history — indeed any subject or concept with which he tried to grapple during the subsequent years of study.

During the first part of his sophomore year the liveliest literary experiences he had were extracurricular. He took a "strong dose of literature," on his own responsibility apparently, reading Frost, Cummings, and Dylan Thomas; *King John, The Turn of the Screw,* and *Mrs. Dalloway.* "Late in the winter I read D. B. Wyndham Lewis's *François Villon,* and was greatly moved by Lewis's own writing and by Villon."

Of his writing that semester he said:

In general, papers were very important to me. Writing well is a great source of satisfaction. When I could choose my own topic, my papers usually represented a direct tackling of my current concerns. Assigned topics usually meant hack-work papers. First term's papers were all of this latter sort.

It was in the second term of that year that the literature he read began to weave itself into the fabric of his education. His reading became a rich source of images and examples giving substance to the ideas he was meeting in all parts of his studies; and it added the sharp imaginative awareness a work of art gives to the ordinary observations of human behavior. From this point on it becomes clear that literature is no longer a "subject" but a means for intensifying any experience he encounters, whatever he is studying.

He apparently had little interest in form or technique. He wrote some poetry, he said, and he read certain modern poets. The meaning of such reading to his life would be hard to discover, and perhaps he does not know himself. What we do know is that he turned very often to literature to find ways of developing or illuminating questions and ideas that occupied his thought. Literature is the opening door for many young people to an understanding of human experience, of personal attachments, of social issues, of man's effort to find and to understand his place in the world; and students are indeed fortunate who early in their expanding college life have an opportunity to study literature in ways that help them discover the light it can cast on their search for such understanding. In this sense literature is perhaps not a discipline at all, but a way of approaching imaginatively questions for which they will have to seek solutions in other fields of learning. Much teaching of literature fails to serve this purpose for students; Scott was fortunate in discovering these uses of literature early in his college years.

A single illustration of how a literary work not only illuminated his thinking when he first read it, but how it grew in meaning as his thinking grew will point out how important literature can become for one who is not a student of literature.

In an American literature course, in his second year, Scott read *Huckleberry Finn,* and it is worth tracing his use of this book through that year and the next.

He first wrote a paper called "Jim and Huck." It is a rather simple paper. Its theme is the friendship between Huck and Jim:

> The relationship between Jim and Huck is in itself a major point in *Huck Finn*. . . . The two are strikingly similar, particularly in being alone against society. Huck's and Jim's search for freedom is indeed a theme here, but Huck and Jim in themselves constitute a theme: Huck alone on the river would be a different story.

He points out that Huck comes more and more under Jim's influence; that early in their relation Huck accepts no responsibility for the snake bite Jim suffers, although he is in fact responsible; that their relation has shifted by the time they discuss boarding the derelict boat — an argument "clearly between equals"; and soon:

> Huck apologizes to Jim for having lied about their separation in the storm. The obligation of honesty which real intimacy entails is deeply felt by Huck; Jim has become human in his mind extraordinarily quickly.

> .   .   .   .

> The protective closeness between Jim and Huck manifests itself in various ways. Huck can lie for Jim and himself, but not for the duke and dauphin. When the duke and dauphin arrive, there are not four people on the raft, but two groups of two. If anything, the duke and dauphin emphasize by contrast what Jim and Huck are: mistrust serves to underline trust, and argument, accord. When Jim is sold by the dauphin Huck's loyalty persists over his new doubts. He defiantly agrees to go to hell for the sin of helping Jim.

He elaborates this theme of the developing friendship to the point at which the friends must separate, and discusses the meaning of their separation.

Scott was disappointed in his teacher's reception of this paper. "It was hard work on my part," he said, "and I was disappointed that the section man didn't like it. It was created entirely by me, that is, with no specific assignment requested in advance, except that it had to deal with Twain's book." Actually the section man was not severely critical. He said the writing was uneven — "your ideas deserve better treatment. You have something to say; so take pains saying it." And his criticism was just — the writing is clumsier than in other papers Scott wrote that year. But the important thing about the paper is that it is the rather limping beginning of an ability both to be critically sensitive to a writer's purpose and to find in the literary work substance for clarifying and developing ideas that were becoming important to Scott. How much he actually discovered by reading this book, and how much the book captured something he was discovering anyhow, it is impossible to say. But it doesn't matter. The book, like his education as a whole, was the occasion for what Bronowski calls the "creative leap" which the writer makes when he creates the writing, and which the reader makes again when the work enlarges his own understanding.

This was the only "original" paper Scott wrote on a literary work as such; but all his papers after this made use — sometimes very large use — of his reading of literature.

Later that year he wrote what he called his most important paper, "Alienation and Alternatives." Its part in his education was discussed earlier. Here it is necessary to mention only the way his reading of literature fed his thinking about this paper and its subject, with which he was preoccupied for many reasons, not the least of which was his effort to find direction for himself.

By the time he came to write "Alienation and Alternatives" his thinking about Huckleberry Finn, the boy and the book, had moved ahead. It is as if he had had the experience one often has with important reading — that, in a way, he had kept on reading the book after he had finished it and even after he had written something about it.

He read Kerouac's *On the Road,* and the two books together gave substance to the point he had to make. What he sees are two kinds of "lone" men — the detached and the alienated.

> Alienation and detachment are seen as bad and good ways, respectively, to be apart, to be a lone man. . . . The detached person is committed positively to certain goals and values . . . the alienated person is crippled, weak, while the detached is strong.
>
> .   .   .   .
>
> Perhaps I can best bring out the differences between the two types of lone men by a comparison of two American novels, Mark Twain's *The Adventures of Huckleberry Finn* and Jack Kerouac's *On the Road.* These two books are closer to being the same book in meaning and implication than any other pair that I have ever noted. Twain's book is indisputably the greater of the two, and in this sense there is no comparison between them. But putting this aside, we see that both novels are devastating criticisms of society made by the existence of a pair of lonely travelers. Each pair is symbolically helpless (riding a raft on the one hand, and hitching rides and stealing cars on the other) and within each there is a significant interaction which may be characterized as the narrator's search for a symbolic father. Such remarkable spiritual affinity between two books is surely rare.
>
> From Twain to Kerouac, there is a slight shift; however, one that makes all the difference. It is, of course, the shift from detachment (Huck) to alienation (Sal). Huck's narration took place in the 1840's and Sal's in the 1940's. The gulf between these two eras is

one of more than time. It is fruitful to see symbolized in the shift from Huck to Sal the larger shift from nineteenth to twentieth century America. Compare for example the relative speeds of a raft and a rushing car. Speed blurs matters considerably: "With frantic Dean I was rushing through the world without a chance to see it." This loss of clarity in the movement from Huck to Sal is part of a larger shift. The key to the character of this shift is to be found in the interaction between Huck and Jim, and Sal and Dean.

One way to characterize this is to point to it as a search for a father, though this theme is not necessarily the final answer. It is a highly plausible interpretation of *Huckleberry Finn,* but is hotly contested by critics. Sal calls Dean "the father we never found," but we may suspect that this is another of Kerouac's many irrelevant remarks about the meaning of being on the road. An arbitrary decision here is unnecessary, for the following pair of sentences are, at any rate, interchangeable conclusions: (1) Huck found in Jim a father, and was thereby enabled to grow up, which Sal, fatherless, could not do; (2) The relationship between Huck and Jim became one of love, giving Huck the strength to become detached, while Sal's relationship with Dean is finally futile, and leaves him essentially a child. The turning points in each relationship are very similar incidents. In each the narrator has abused the integrity of the companion, causing the latter to turn away in anger and with injured pride. Sal, realizing he had acted wrongly, whines to Dean: "It's not my fault, don't you see that?" Huck, rather than refusing to take the blame, accepts entire responsibility for his act:

> "It was fifteen minutes before I could work myself up to go and humble myself to a nigger; but I done it, and I warn't ever sorry for it afterward, neither. I didn't do him no more mean tricks, and I wouldn't done that one if I'd 'a' knowed it would make him feel that way."

Huck feels, as Sal does, the obligation of honesty which real intimacy entails. So Huck, who has rejected society in accepting Jim, is able to close his narrative in fulfillment:

> "But I reckon I got to light out for the Territory ahead of the rest, because Aunt Sally she's going to adopt me and sivilize me, and I can't stand it. I been there before."

Sal, who has been left in the middle of nowhere, closes his narrative in futility, daydreaming about "Old Dean Moriarty, the father we never found."

Scott has read a good deal, and his reading is alive and at his call. In talking about his high school studies he mentioned books that had impressed him, and, among them, Shirley Jackson's short stories. Here he goes back to one of them, rediscovering it, as he had rediscovered Huck Finn. The characters in the short story "Colloquy," he says, "are indeed alienated from society and their case reveals how intolerable is this state. Given this discomfort, it follows that something must be done. Some answers, some alternatives must be sought." Kerouac "has nothing to offer us in the way of a solution but the shoulder-shrugging impotence." Norman Mailer "romanticizes alienation . . . declares that living in this moment-to-moment uncertainty takes courage." But Scott cannot accept that either. "This is not actually courage, but a variation on the general helplessness of the alienated person. . . . Courage consists in part of taking a stand when it may be the wrong one." So he has to reject the analysis of such writers.

He turns to literature to support his own attempt to find alternatives in a world which many searching people cannot accept, and uses the case of Odysseus, in Nikos Kazantzakis's *The Odyssey: a Modern Sequel,* as one alternative. He thinks of this as:

> a more successful expression of that which Mailer attempted, the courageous transformation of the running away into running toward.

> . . . .

> We may speak of Kazantzakis's Odysseus as alienated, but such a designation hardly does justice to his character. . . . The modern Odysseus is a man who cannot settle down to comfortable virtues and betray the restless search. Traveling through the western Mediterranean, Africa, and the Antarctic, Odysseus attempts to live so fully that eventual Death will have nothing to take from him.

Scott has to debate with himself whether this sort of escape from rootlessness is a legitimate one for a man not a mythical hero, and has to cope with the question Sapir raised about the "helplessness of the individual who has no cultural heritage to work on." He knows *this* is no real solution.

He ranges among the literature he has been reading for evidence of "the other exceptional solution to alienation — artistic creativity" — and finds Virginia Woolf on the apartness of the artist, Hawthorne (whom he had read the previous year in an American literature course) in the years of his early solitude. He finds in the *Notebooks* a passage about Hawthorne's lonely youth:

> If ever I should have a biographer, he ought to make great mention of this chamber in my memoirs, because so much of my lonely youth was wasted here, and here my mind and character were formed; and here I have been glad and hopeful, and here I have been despondent. . . . By and by the world found me out in my

lonely chamber, and called me forth — not indeed with a loud roar of acclamation, but with a still small voice — and forth I went, but found nothing in the world I thought preferable to my solitude till now. . . . And now I begin to understand why I was imprisoned so many years in this lonely chamber, and why I could never break through the viewless bolts and bars; for if I had sooner made my escape into the world, I should have grown hard and rough, and been covered with earthly dust, and my heart might have become callous by rude encounters with the multitude.

He turns to Henry Miller's *To Paint Is to Love Again,* an account of the pleasures in the effort of painting, the experience of seeing the object, the pleasure of the finished picture:

Just how great a compensation for alienation creativity can be to the artist is illustrated by Miller's remark that if he had not discovered painting as an outlet, he probably would have gone insane.

Critics, research men, artists, find in their creativity ways of compensating for alienation, so that aloneness is no longer sterile.

In this sophomore year, as the rest of his work and his comments on it indicate, Scott was involved in the effort to deal with how an individual can live a desirable life in relation to a society of which he does not feel himself a part — the need neither to conform nor to "alienate" oneself. He was reaching out in all directions, in his reading, to find possible solutions to this need, and he seemed to be working positively at it. Here literature came to his aid, although much more of his reading was outside the field of pure literature.

As the general account indicates, and as he says himself, "everything fell apart at the beginning of the Junior year" — and this was evident in an interview with him in January of that year. The largest service literature performed for him seems to have been during the months he was trying to clarify this matter of the individual's self-definition in relation to society. The emphasis of the year in his studies was in psychology, and he was, I think, projecting his own effort at self-understanding in writing these papers.

By the time he worked his way through the confusion of the junior year — confusion which was focused on what *he* should do as a potential conscientious objector, what position *he* should take on disarmament, how *he* could function in relation to movements for peace, and so on — his central interest was turned from himself to problems of politics. The contrast between his paper on crime early in that year and the one on Hoover at the end of the year — both the subjects and his attitude toward them — illustrate what had happened in the interval to his thinking. Neither says much about literature. In the Hoover paper he speaks of only one creative writer and he makes only one literary reference (one that, had he dealt with his problem as subjectively as he had dealt with earlier problems, would certainly have lent itself to literary analogy). This paper is discussed in the previous chapter for the light it throws on the changes going on in Scott's thinking about politics and his relation to the political structure, and it is there pointed out that, in a way, his close attention to Hoover and to Hoover's imprisonment in his "ideology" may have been a device for forcing him to think about his own efforts to develop an ideology and about his conclusion that this is not the way he should cope with his questions. The one literary reference in the Hoover paper is to Thomas Wolfe:

> One usually senses a certain embarrassment at political gatherings in speaker and audience when the speaker refers to the American way of life. There is an immense intuitive love for America in most Americans, but this is something *non-ideological* which cannot be used for political purposes. An author like Thomas Wolfe demonstrates this intuitive patriotism well. . . . Thomas Wolfe was not patriotic in a nationalistic sense; his was rather a thorough love of the processes of living in America — as I say, an intuitive patriotism.

The novel that seems to have been important during the time he was deciding that he could not use the ideal of disarmament, or pacifism, or conscientious objection as his platform for coping with dangers and dislocations without knowing much more than he knew at that point, was Robert Penn Warren's *All the King's Men.*

Literature continues to be a moving force in his feeling and thought. He speaks of:

> a strong affection for individual people, for different aspects of the human condition. It's a vague principle that explains my strong reaction to such books as Paton's *Cry, the Beloved Country, Child of Our Time,* by Michel del Castillo, James Agee's *Let Us Now Praise Famous Men,* Kamala Markandaya's *Nectar in a Sieve,* Edmund Love's *Subways are for Sleeping,* and Steichen's photo collection *The Family of Man.*

Literature does not provide the main substance of his reading or his thought, but its evocative value is strong. In his senior year his attention turned to writers and other intellectuals who took action in a revolution when they left England to participate in the Spanish Civil War. It was the history of their direct action that interested him; his interest was an interest in them as men, not as writers.

III

Margaret Weaver at Macalester College

SCOTT HANSEN was a "seeker." He may not have known he was one, before he entered Harvard — and perhaps not even afterward. But the story of his education as an undergraduate is a record of his discovery of things he needed to know, and of the sometimes halting, sometimes blind, sometimes quite direct effort to find out something about them. Harvard did not remake Scott's character — whatever turned his attention toward finding out first about himself, and then about the world, was doubtless there when he came to Harvard. Again, we cannot talk about causes, but only about occasions. But certainly his approach to his education and the character of his interest in learning shifted when he faced a new world of intellectual possibilities in his earliest experience as an undergraduate. From then on education became a search and an exploration. It began to consolidate in his senior year when he was able to say "I need competence badly," and realized that he needed to study politics and history. Up to that time he was not principally interested in subject matter or disciplines, although he worked in several different disciplines and met the requirements of most of them on a good or very good level. He was interested in issues or problems or questions. His interest in subject matter really became serious when he decided he could not deal with the questions that interested him most without knowing history and politics.

Like Scott, Margaret Weaver was intelligent; like him she had a very good school record; like him she had strong motivation for study and had demonstrated that she could study. Both came to college thinking they knew where they were headed. For him college opened up large possibilities for life and thought he had not conceived of; for her college intensified and sharpened a way of life and thought already pretty fully directed when she came. For him education was an experience first of self- and social discovery — his studies were an instrument in that experience. For her education was an experience in learning more, and more accurately, and with sounder competence, subjects that had been important to her to begin with. The story of her education is the story of how she used the college, the environment, and the opportunities offered by the college, or wrung from it by her insistence, for that end. It is a story of how her interest in government and politics was fed and informed by what she studied and the life she was able to design in and out of the college. Like Scott Hansen, and unlike many bright, acquisitive students, the progress of her interest and the accumulation of knowledge was accompanied by an almost continuous stream of speculation, question, reflection, and position-taking about what she learned.

More than that, there is an interesting development in her ideas and values relating to matters that are certain to be central to whatever life she might be thinking about as a lawyer, politician, office holder, or active citizen. For instance, in papers written throughout her undergraduate years she returns many times to the question of how much and what kind of authority either the state or an individual in possession of power should wield. Her academic history, in which learning about government and politics is basic, is also a record of increasing interest in such central questions as this one — what issues will affect her position, what attitude toward social organization, human nature, the nature of law and of official and public responsibility she will take, on whatever problem is under discussion or inquiry. She had a label or description of herself. What the description means, or whether it indicates where she will stand or what her values will be ten years from now is another question. She called herself a liberal democrat; and she used college assignments to explore her beliefs and state them many times. If her intellectual life continues to be as active as it is now, it will be interesting to watch where she comes out on the issue of power, and what leads her there.

In her college application Margaret Weaver said she either wanted to be a political science teacher or go into politics, because "if honest and capable people do not go into politics, dishonest people will." At that time she said she wanted to go to law school.

She described herself as coming from a lower-middle-class family "in a commuter and very Republican suburb" of Chicago, the eldest of six children in a family without interest in college education. Her own interest in learning and her curiosity about world events came from somewhere in her childhood and adolescence, but she cannot, she says, attribute it to family background "as these were not primary values in my family." What living in her family did create was a strong sense of independence. "Both because of the nature of my home life and because I came from a large family, independence was necessary to survival."

With no further knowledge of her background than these remarks provide, it is obvious that she early developed a species of in-spite-of-the-roadblocks determination.

This quality was characteristic of her behavior all through college — of the ways she worked, the way she carved out her private curriculum, the way she lived, the relations she had with the faculty. She conveyed, at first meeting, a strong conviction that she must, somehow, be herself — that other people had ideas about what she, or any proper college student, ought to be, but that she was not willing to succumb to these ideas.

This girl did not engage in the kind of speculations and self-searching inquiries that occupied Scott Hansen. There is nothing utopian about her; she has a stainless-steel quality; she is impatient; she does not want to be one of the crowd; she is self-interested, intolerant of inadequate teaching, and of inadequacy generally. She is not an easily reached person. But she has both a strong social conscience, and strong convictions about what education should accomplish for the life and the values of individuals, and she wants to make no compromise with justice as she sees it.

"I Want to Be a Senator"

A POLITICAL science professor with whom Margaret Weaver studied at the college said that the first time he saw her was a day she walked into his office and said "I want to be a senator, and I should probably start now."

This is a characteristically direct approach of a bright girl who has had to make her own way, whose determination and (in the opinion of some people who know her) intolerance lie on the surface. "She is never going to do much of anything she doesn't want to do," a professor said, "and with her talents and energy, she should not have to."

She graduated with a double major in political science and economics, having completed college in three years. She was on a partial scholarship from the beginning, and worked to pay for the rest of her expenses.

She spoke with respect and affection of her high school, where classes and individual teachers encouraged her and fostered in her the desire for achievement. She learned in this suburban school not only tools to use but values to explore that helped her use college to advantage:

> I learned to study and enjoy studying for its own sake; and I learned the feeling of excitement that comes when you dig into a subject, or find the key to a thought that has been in the back of your mind.

It was in high school that her interest in affairs of the world, in the social sciences began:

> The more I read and studied, the more liberal my political and social outlook became until, in the last two years of high school, I found myself one of the two student Democrats in the school.

Looking back from the end of her college years, she believes that "the beginnings of my values and social ideas and ideals were embedded in me" in those years, but these were only dimly conceived, and it was in college that she began to learn what was involved in holding the beliefs that had begun to take shape, how they affected all aspects of life, what questions to ask about them.

In the last year of high school she came across Russell's *History of Western Philosophy* and some books on Indian philosophy. She was not captivated by Indian philosophy (as many students are in the late high school and early college years), but she mentions this reading in passing as the first that turned her thoughts to moral and ethical matters. "I don't believe I'd thought about them until then. These books stimulated my thinking, but left it mainly for college to develop."

She speaks of an early interest in music, which seems to have been serious in the high school years. "I played in nearly every band and orchestra the high school offered, and several others they did not." She never mentioned what instruments she played. She won a scholarship to a music camp the summer of her junior year.

The feelings of young people who work in mental hospitals (and music takes a good many into them) are often deeply engaged by the experience, and they envision a use for themselves in music therapy. So it was with her. It seemed to her a "wonderful and rewarding field for service." But the sense of her own intellectual needs was strong even then, and when she found that the programs of the schools training for this work offered almost no chance to study anything beyond music and the necessary science and medical courses, she decided against it. There was still too much to learn about the politics and economics she had begun thinking about in high school, and she started then to consider college.

She had no financial resources, but, in spite of this, rejected the state colleges in Illinois as "not having a very good reputation" to her way of thinking. Northwestern, the University of Chicago, Lawrence, Carleton, and St. Olaf's were the colleges she was interested in. Money stood in the way in some cases, uncertainty about what kind of work in political science and economics she would find in others. One reason for turning from St. Olaf's was that the regulations were too strict.

A high school teacher suggested Macalester. People spoke with respect of the work in social science there — she apparently inquired closely about the college. She was offered a scholarship and decided to go to Macalester:

> I don't know what I expected when I came. Now I might say that I expected to continue my high-school learning, prepare for graduate school, and somehow, through learning, become a better person.

The "Fit" of the Student and the College

WHY this college — and why this list of possibilities? How students select colleges, and from what range of possibilities, is something of a mystery even to the most thoroughly initiated, and the process by which institutions become possibilities to a particular student from a particular high school is obviously full of accidents. The possibilities this student had before her were all within fairly close geographical range of her home, although being close to home probably mattered less to her than to many college freshmen. None of the Eastern "elite" colleges, apparently, was in the picture as a possibility, although she probably would have done well in any one of them. She would have met the intellectual challenge of colleges more selective in their admissions procedures than the college she chose. Had she gone to one of the Eastern women's colleges she would have been academically successful, and probably restless in an all-female student body.

But talking with her when she was ready to end her college years, I felt that, however accidental, the choice had been a good one for her. She had certainly extracted everything she could from the college she had found her way to, and it is possible that she had had a better period of learning and growth than she might have had if somebody had picked her up and put her in one of the "name" colleges of the East. I suggest that both the general climate of Macalester College (although in many ways she was critical of it) and the particular opportunities it provided for her to function in a way congenial to her mind and her nature, were positive factors in her education and made the choice of this college a good one for her.

It was important to her to be able to have a feeling of "grasp" — the feeling that she knows something about the situation she finds herself in, in the terms that interest her most — political problems and political organization. Possibly she would not have found so readily at another college, in another place, the chance to do the kind of grass-roots study and work she found it quite easy to get into in Minneapolis and St. Paul, once the college recognized what she was like and gave her her head. The state legislature was right there. She found problems involving the administration of law and social justice at her doorstep, and she could in the most natural and appropriate way become involved in these problems.

Discussing her education six months after she had finished college and was nearing the end of her first semester in law school, she said that even if she had had the chance to go to a private Eastern college she would have chosen to stay in her own part of the country. She had not been especially impressed, she said, by the girls from the Eastern women's colleges she had met, and looking back she did not feel that their education had been better than hers:

> The only college I would like to have gone to, with the hindsight I have, would be Antioch. . . . Because of . . . the combination of work and study; and their school program is quite independent, and very liberal and broad.

As we talked about students in Eastern colleges she asked whether I thought they were interested in "using" their education — or "are they just interested in going to college for their own sakes?" She thought most of the people she knew expected to use their education in some way. "Even the girls who come to some extent to get married usually go into teaching or something. A lot of ex-Mac students have gone into Peace Corps work — there must have been five or six of them just this year."

A single objective can be traced from the comments in her high school application to the college, through the papers she wrote, through the turn of her conversation in interviews toward the end of her college life, to her reflections on her education six months out of college. How to get the most education she could, how to understand its implications for her thought about politics and law, and how to use what she got in practical ways, were all bound up in her thought and action, and were responsible for the way she took hold of her own education and directed it as fully as she was permitted to do.

She was not an easy student to teach — at least not for all teachers. She has an impatient and restless nature, she has a vivid sense of the importance of time — so much to learn, so little time — and, on the face of it, little tolerance, as one professor put it, for "courses and material which she considers to be mickey-mouse." She raised mixed feelings in her teachers — although it was clear in her high school days and later that she reveres teachers who will understand her and reach out to feed a sharp appetite for learning. A political science professor said of her: "Her intellectual resources are enormous, and when combined with her capacity to concentrate and to focus her interests, cannot help but lead to outstanding academic and professional success. She has a wonderful sense of humor and at times those whom she does not respect find themselves on the receiving end of her levity. To me she was always a real challenge and a fascinating debate partner."

Others thought that she "has great intellectual ability, but needs more guidance than she realizes." Another reports that "her idea of what should constitute the course she registered for was not the way the course was being taught." He discussed the course with her, at her initiative. "This changed her mind not at all, and produced only a gradual change in her attitude from open hostility to armed truce."

While the college did not create her interest in politics and government, it gave unusual scope for its development. And other students at this college spoke of this aspect of the life there. Another senior, speaking of the interest of students in national and international affairs, talked of how such interest was fostered, more than it is fostered in other places:

> Take X College, for instance — the academic standards are high and the students very good, and they do very good work. But they are more private, and what they are interested in is more private than it is here. More people here, among the good students, are really interested in domestic political and international affairs. It may have something to do with the large number of foreign students — but it can't be just that, because other places that have foreign students aren't like this. I have friends who were interested in the same things I was, in high school, who have gone other places and have given them up. Some of them are most interested now in jobs and vocational things, and they don't talk about pol-

itics or such matters any more. At Y University, for instance, several friends went there, and they have a lot of foreign students there, but there isn't the same interest in those students, or in foreign affairs there is here — although some of them would like to have found that.

There were, in fact, many foreign students in the college during these years, and good opportunities were provided there for work and study abroad for many students. Elsewhere I have discussed SPAN and other activities of this college (pages 167–168) which combine regular academic studies with foreign work and study programs. There is a strong political science influence in the faculty, especially in the person of one professor, whose name came up repeatedly, even when students did not like his ideas, or were critical of his ways. Students planning to study law, students interested in state politics or national affairs, students preparing for graduate school and college teaching, Americans who had participated in the college's foreign-study programs and foreign students from emerging countries interested in studying political theory and political organization spoke of his effect on their thinking:

> From the beginning he insists in his teaching that conflict is a norm — that conflict is part of the nature of human organization, that understanding politics and government and the way people relate to each other in institutions has to take this into account. He deals with all sorts of issues which involve conflict and builds up a whole network of ideas which people have to consider in relation to each other, and in relation to this view of his. He keeps telling us that social and political conflicts do not become fully and correctly resolved — you arrive at a partial or temporary solution and what you have to be concerned about is that these temporary and partial solutions are the best you can make at the time — and be ready to go at them again.

"I Was Lucky That First Year"

MARGARET had an exciting and profitable freshman year:

> I was lucky that first year. By chance I found myself in two of the best courses I was to have in my years at Macalester, rather than in the usual array of introductory courses. A course in history was taught in a way to inspire even the worst student in the class, and to make all of us want to work and work hard. There were no formal lectures. We discussed the weekly papers students wrote on the current reading assignments and on extra readings. A list of topics

— generally speculative questions — were handed out covering each area. These were not only fun to write and think about, but often provided starting points for very interesting discussions.

The second course was an upper-division course in French 19th century literature. There were only eight of us in the class and the professor made us all feel her enthusiasm for France and France's literature. This class, too, was primarily discussions of the works we read.

This student exhibited in all her comments about her education a probing interest in what happens in the educational process.

She returned several times to that experience of the freshman year; and in a paper written in her senior year in which she reviewed her own education she wrote:

These courses reinforced the interest in study and academic work I brought with me from high school; and I can only say that incoming freshmen should all have courses like these. It seems to me the job of colleges in the first year — to reinforce or help build this internal motivation.

One hopes that in a college like this one exposure to all kinds of courses and subjects will "reach" students in one area or another, but this hope is often disappointed. I know that the subject area, the type of course, the method of teaching, are all matters that depend on the talents and tastes of professors and students.

She apparently read a good deal of literature then and later; she still does, she says, but there is in her writing and her later comments none of the evidence that imaginative literature, then or now, was absorbed into her thought and feeling about the ideas that interest her, as there is in the case of Scott Hansen. There is little evidence of aesthetic interests and her talk draws little on her reading of literature. The papers from that first literature course are revealing both of her tenacity in her way of looking at the world and of her analytical mind. Writing about Balzac she says "My primary purpose is to see the social species represented, rather than just to present a character sketch"; and she is far more reluctant to make a critical judgment about a literary position than she ever is about other matters. There is little evidence in her writing or her talk that literature is part of her life and thought, and her literary judgments are not impressive. She likes to read novels and discuss them — perhaps they remain the subject of small talk in her life.

There is much more substantial evidence of what she accomplished that year in the study of history. It was a course in Modern European History, beginning with a study of the rise of mercantilism and ending with the defeat of Nazism. Whether this course gave a turn to her thinking that persisted through her college years, or whether (and more likely) it dealt with political history in a way especially congenial to her, it is not possible to say. But the design of the course — or at least the part of the material she put her energies into — gave her experience in thinking about the question of power — a question that occupied her many times in her studies; a question that either shapes or reflects the cast of her mind.

The course required a paper each week. These papers are typically three to four typewritten pages long, and they not only indicate the subject matter and orientation of the course, but reveal her own concerns as, from week to week, she selected topics to write on. The course was carefully planned by the teacher. Syllabus, reading lists, topics for papers, were in the hands of the students, regular performance was called for, papers were carefully read. This external structure went along, apparently, with a good deal of freedom in the conduct of classes — she still looked back, at the end of the college years, to the opportunities to discuss, and to the teacher's interest in ideas and in the implications for contemporary life of the subjects a rather formal course provided.

There was evidently a good standard set for the weekly papers. Faced with such regular demands for writing, students often allow their writing to become routine, but Margaret did not. Her first paper was "A Critique of Mercantilism," listing all the characteristics of that era — a factual report, brief, but full of information about the nature of mercantilism and its usefulness for the time. From the first, though, her papers show an interest in the relation of whatever historical issue she is studying to current ones:

> Mercantilist beliefs have persisted to the present time in the form of arguments and policies for a favorable balance of trade. There are many strong arguments to show the fallacies of such thinking, yet these very policies encouraged countries at that time to aid colonies in getting started, and aid business, industry, and trade in becoming a well-established part of the life today.

In the first few papers, however, she was mainly reporting on her reading. By the middle of October she begins to make judgments, already concerning herself with causes, already coping with the question of the relation of the government to the people, of the ruler to the government and to the people, that occupies her in some form all through her education. The ability to pack a good deal of reporting into short space stays with her, but she begins to be occupied with the meaning of the historical movements she reports.

Later papers that semester have such titles as "How and Why Did Prussia Rise to Power?"; "Why Did a Fundamental and Violent Revolution Occur in France?"; "Why Was Japan Able To Beat Russia in the Russo-Japanese War?"; and a review of all her writing throughout her college years shows her titles (and her mind) often asking, "Why?"

That year she wrote on the "Nature and Power of Nationalism," a paper typical of the way her thoughts were turned then and later. Here she lists, in her usual swift way, a long series of factors that may create or intensify nationalistic feeling, but are not sufficient or even necessary to it. Here, as elsewhere, she shows the tendency to list everything she can think of that might apply to the subject she is defining or argue for the point she is making — a classifying habit which many bright students have, but which is not really of much use, intellectually, unless they proceed beyond it to analysis — which she does from the beginning, and more and more as time goes on.

If something else, beyond these factors, is necessary to produce nationalism, what is needed? "The one thing that is called for above all others is will. An active will is needed to unite a majority behind nationalism." She provides a swift account of the development of nationalism through the increase of feeling of the middle class that it had a stake in government, elimination of class privilege, the slogans, the declaration of the Rights of Man, the crumbling of orthodox religion in Europe, allowing for the transfer of allegiance from church to state, the importance of the idea of citizenship, the spread of common language through education, national conscription, which also gave people the feeling of participation in the affairs of the country, and so on, and then goes on to say:

> The main outlet of nationalism would of course be politics. The first noticeable effects were in movements and unrest leading toward independence. . . . After strong national states were formed and unification was evident, the forces of nationalism had to be diverted along other lines, leading, in the case of the European powers, to imperialism. Although the main reasons for imperialism were economic, the main justifications were humanitarian and nationalistic. In most colonies the people were not protected from economic exploitation, but were being taught the European ideals

and methods of governing. This inculcation of ideals is what is turning nationalism in Asia against colonial powers today.

The point of quoting this paper, is that it is the first of many efforts in the papers she wrote, the courses she took, the independent study she worked out, to deal with the question of the nature and source of power in governments. She wrote, in that course, on "British Rule in India after the Sepoy Mutiny of 1857." After an account of the steps in the establishment of British power in India, she points out:

> The second half of the eighteenth century until the first half of the nineteenth is the story of the British conquest; after that the main theme is one of the rise of Indian nationalism.

Describing the process by which the British government took over the rule of India, and proceeded with the process of westernizing India, making changes in education, the court system, public health:

> What does all this mean in terms of the British rule and the beginnings of the Indian independence movement? . . . The central government contributed uniformity and efficiency, but in serving these ends, forgot about any Indian self-rule. They were highminded and strove to do the best they could for the people of India, but they failed to realize that the people of India might want to start doing things for themselves. In fact it was their very own doing that the people of India were educated in the principles of self-government, but not able to practice them.

Her final papers for that course were on Nazi doctrine, and on Japanese imperialism, and in both she again is principally interested in how governments get, wield, and keep power. It is probably the most persistent issue in her developing thought about government.

She lists as the principal issues in Nazi doctrine:

> If there are these doctrines, then an organization of government is needed to carry them into effect. The organization, of course, is a dictatorship. . . . It is interesting to note that, in this authoritarian type of regime, parliaments were considered necessary (ideally). They were to act as councilors (although the final word was always with one man), and they were to be the proving ground for the rise of leaders. . . . [Hitler] regarded two groups of philosophies of peoples. These were the nationalists and the socialists, who are considered to be opposites by most people. Hitler saw in these two groups a common fight and identity of two ideals. This he puts very succinctly, "The purest form of socialism signifies the conscious

elevation of the claims and interests of the life of the people over the interests and claims of the individual . . . the highest form of nationalism finds expression only in the unconditional devotion of the individual to the people."

.   .   .   .

Hitler recognized the greater efficiency of a small group of fanatics than a large group of just supporters.

.   .   .   .

Education served to build up idealism and emotionalism rather than intellectualism. The purpose of this is the simple psychology that faith is less easily shaken than education. Emotionalism and excitement control beliefs much more effectively than intellectual acceptance of an idea. Intellectual acceptance leads more readily to apathy and indifference, the chief foes of any movement, while emotionalism leads to action and unquestioning following.

"They Let Me Even When It Was a Little Illegal": The Chance for Independent Study

THE educational life of a student who is using the college years to the full for learning is very complicated. I have selected to describe two of the most important aspects of this student's education as illustrative of what the college permitted as an educational institution; what its climate or style of life encouraged; and how she used the opportunities she had. These two aspects of her education are the rather extraordinary opportunities for independent study the college made possible, and the basic connections the student made between her theoretical studies and the life of the political world around her that she came to know during these years.

Macalester College gave Margaret Weaver large opportunities for working in her own way, and learning by her own design. She studied language and literature, geology and physics, religion, psychology, and philosophy. She was interested in education and several times used the assignment of papers as opportunities for saying what she thought — about the purposes of education, the assets and liabilities in the way her own college designed education, in what needed doing, as she saw it. She wrote a psychology paper on learning, and used it to discuss ways of teaching that gave the student a chance to "internalize his motives for learning."

She wrote not only on psychology and on education; her principal independent study involved work off campus and in seminars and

classes in government and politics; and she obviously thought it important for all students to do more work in these fields. The papers she
wrote as a result of her combination of off-campus and on-campus
work were perhaps the most serious contributions to her education. The
college allowed a great deal of flexibility for this talented girl, permitting her to design her education to a far greater degree than would have
been possible in some institutions. In a letter about her life there she
wrote:

> In a way Macalester is two schools. Formally, it is a fairly strict
> college with traditional courses, though a wide range of these. In-
> formally, however, for those who are willing or able to take advan-
> tage of it, Macalester is much different. There are numerous ways
> for a student to make private arrangements with a professor to
> take a course individually or to do extra independent work. To
> some extent this is also provided for formally by allowing seminar
> courses for upperclassmen who have some specific project in mind.

Having been allowed great leeway, it is not surprising that she says
it is hard to separate what she took from Macalester, and what from related activities:

> I find them all complementary. For instance, Minnesota is an
> unusual state in its variety of people, industries, problems and pol-
> itics. It is exceptionally open to all who come to help or to work. In
> my own experience I found Minnesota politics especially intri-
> guing, and during my second year at Macalester became a research
> assistant to the liberals in the Minnesota House of Representa-
> tives. This was fascinating work dealing with many aspects of Min-
> nesota. I became acquainted with its problems, its people, and its
> politicians. My experience in the House and the contacts I made
> there complemented much of my school work, and, of course, my
> school work greatly helped me in my outside work.

From the time she entered college the interests she brought with
her in politics and government determined the serious direction of her
intellectual life. In discussing the life and education of undergraduates,
in a paper on education, she spoke of the importance of extracurricular
activities the college provided for interested students:

> Some of the better ones are probably the political-emphasis
> week and the religion-in-life weeks, as far as stimulating thought
> and participation on the part of the students in wrestling with the
> problems and responsibilities of citizenship and a philosophy for
> life. There are, of course, many other clubs appealing to all types

of interests. These are good if students use them moderately, but not just to take up every spare hour. Some of the student activities in the last few years on civil rights and other important issues have taught participants a lot about the world and its realities and about the work of service. On-campus activities should be limited to some extent though, and the facilities of the Twin Cities area stressed. Churches, political parties, service clubs, recreation, etc., are all part of the Twin Cities community and should be used by the students to keep in contact with the rest of the non-college world and to broaden their experience and acquaintances. I have learned more about politics and political dynamics in the semester I spent working at the State Capitol and with the Democratic Party than I would have learned in ten years of classes at Macalester. This type of experience is invaluable and should be concomitant with a formal college education. There is not enough stress on these community activities on the Macalester campus among the broad groups of students.

Several times she was permitted to register for regular courses and to carry on the work of the courses independently while holding down a research job for the Minnesota House of Representatives — this is the work she refers to as especially valuable in her education. For the courses she did not attend, she studied the regular textbooks, read extra materials, and wrote papers. She took a course in international economics this way and sat for three two-hour examinations on the course at the end of the term. She had periodical conferences with professors about problems and ideas she met in these studies. She wrote papers on subjects related to the research she was doing in the House of Representatives, and took examinations on the work she had done.

She made two important studies during her undergraduate years, both of which greatly advanced her own knowledge of her field, and had independent importance, beyond their academic importance to her. One of these studies had to do with a proposed amendment to the state constitution which would fix the level of taxes on taconite, a beneficiated form of ore superior for blast-furnace use. The industry is important to the state, and the Republican party and the Republican governor were working to have the tax solidified by constitutional amendment. The Democratic-Farmer-Labor party fought the amendment and Margaret Weaver was engaged to do research on the problem and make a report. The document she wrote became official ammunition of the opponents of the amendment, which was defeated. For purposes of Margaret's intellectual history it is worth noting that apart from the specific reasons she offered against this particular amendment, she wrote with spirit against burdening a constitution with specific issues such as this one:

> It is a matter of general agreement among lawyers and constitutional experts that the constitution, as a document, ought not to be rendered inflexible through the addition of numerous amendments that could just as easily and better be legislatively enacted. Matters of policy should be decided by deliberative bodies within the broad framework of the constitution. And, since conditions and perspectives change over the passage of time, such legislative policy can be altered to meet new situations and challenges. The example of Louisiana and California should prove warning enough against writing lengthy and inflexible constitutions . . . the constitution is a sacred document, not a Persian market place for bartering and bargaining. The power to tax has long been a legislative prerogative. This amendment would limit that power of the legislature.

While she was working at the State House a redistricting bill had been passed involving a district that had had an important history in the political life of the state. She undertook a "district analysis" of this area for the purpose of providing information, ideas, and proposals about campaigning in the new district. The study served also to meet course requirements in the political science department.

The paper she wrote gives testimony to the development of the political leanings that, years earlier, had made her one of the two Democrats in her high school, and it is part of her preparation for the career that will follow:

> This area . . . is not a "typical" rural area, if indeed there is such a thing. It is the area in our state which has been the home of most of the independent protest movements which have swept the scene from time to time, and its politics are geared to an electorate of independent thinkers with liberal leanings, but who will vote for a man before a party. They are fairly pragmatic in both their liberalism and their conservatism. In a sense they are a class of "Engine Charley" Wilsons who say that what is good for the farmer and for me is good for the country. Perhaps this is one reason for choosing this district as it is historically, spiritually, and ideologically sort of the writer's second home.
>
> .   .   .   .
>
> The Seventh District is not a statistic. It has a personality and spirit which defied quantitative analysis. Its spirit is to be found in the history of the State of Minnesota and of the rural protest movement which periodically sprang up to fight real or imagined abuses. The Seventh District has been the home and breeding place

of most of the independent parties and protest movements that have become so much a part of our heritage. The first requisite, therefore, of a "district analysis" is to review briefly the unique and fascinating historical background of the northwestern portion of our state.

This history of rural protest movements can only be viewed as an educational process for the farmer — an intensive "short course" in the economics and politics of our country. The learning method was not didactic, but empirical. Armed with the American ideals of freedom and opportunity, the farmers saw themselves become poor pawns in a growing industrial economy and sought to right or to alleviate their distress by a series of repair jobs on the economic system. They tried working through established political parties, but found these controlled by the same people they were fighting or had picked as scapegoats. They then took one step to the left and tried independent political action. The educational process was a painful one; learning often came through tragic mistakes and involved suffering and disillusionment, but the farmers did learn. They learned and elected a Farmer-Labor Governor in 1932 by the name of Floyd B. Olson. This of course did not solve their problems, but it was the depression payoff of a hard educational process.

Floyd Olson's Farmer-Labor Party was the apostolic successor to the Grangers, the Populists, the Greenbackers, and other groups. The many groups and their frequent rebirth attest to the prolonged distress of the rural community which accompanied the change from a frontier community to a complex interdependent economy.

.   .   .   .

All these things, these sociological factors, these intangibles, were brought home again and again to the writer in a tour of the Seventh District, both in interviewing people and in observing and talking to whoever happened to be available for conversation at gas stations, cafes, motels, etc. The approach of the farmer today is essentially the same as yesterday. He votes and thinks pragmatically on the basis of what he thinks is right or on what he thinks is good for the farmer. An interesting example of this pragmatism occurred while the writer was sitting in Representative Victor Johnson's newspaper office in Lake Bronson. An old farmer walked in to sign up for a turkey drawing and to say hello. His comment after formalities to Representative Johnson was "Glad to see the special session was short. I saw in the paper this morning how much that costs a day. That's terrible expensive!" The comment had nothing to do with the all-important issue of redistricting accomplished, but only with the cost of the session. On explanation of what was accomplished, the farmer agreed that it certainly was a necessary session and a good thing — but he was still glad that it was short.

Her sources are largely primary — interviews with candidates, members of the Farmers' Union, DFL party workers, newspaper men, potential candidates, district leaders, congressmen, and just individuals. Also the printed election laws, the census, voting records, constitutions of the parties concerned.

It was a grass-roots inquiry, and an important contribution to her education. Many students, if they could carry on their education in an environment that actively engaged them, would find a reality and importance in their college years, as this girl did, which too many now fail to find.

"There Is No Universal Truth. There May Be Only Universal Questions"

IT was not only in her independent studies that her interest in contemporary political life found exercise. She had a talent for finding in general, historical, theoretical ideas immediate application to the matters that occupied her about current life. We cannot speak of this as a "practical" as against an "intellectual" interest. It is not even a fusion of practical and theoretical interests; there is a unity in her intellectual life worth considering as we speculate on the quality of students' thinking. A recent report on Reed College speaks of the "intellectual purpose" of that college — it is described as a home for intellectuals who are not concerned with practical issues; and indeed we have a way of classifying colleges, or subjects in such terms as these. Margaret Weaver's education could not be divided in this way.

She wrote a paper on "Aristotle's Concept of Revolutions." Her discussion of the causes he gives for revolution leads to direct application of his analysis to the American Revolution, the Civil War, and the Russian Revolution. She analyses the question of the corruptibility of magistrates and extends his discussion to problems peculiar to a democratic state. She comes right down to the behavior of Senator Humphrey in relation to the people of her own state. She wrote a paper on John Locke, beginning with the statement that "John Locke is without doubt a classic liberal," and rejects him as a liberal in today's terms:

We must apply his works today as they are being applied and relied upon, and they are to be found largely in the conservative camp. Locke would find today that a great deal of power has been vested in the executive, although today's liberal would answer that this power is accountable — and any President running for reelection would probably agree. Locke would also find that the great and chief end of government, the preservation of property, has been circumvented in many cases by welfarist, or, if you like, socialist schemes for redistribution of wealth as the meanest aim, and for the dignity of human beings as the highest. If Locke's philosophy were assumed to remain static, he could probably write another *Conscience of a Conservative,* although he would undoubtedly do a better and more convincing job.

.   .   .   .

And although Locke found in his love affair with nature that property rights were natural rights, liberals today have tended to come to the realization that the natural policy of government under Locke — laissez-faire — is rather anarchistic and needs to be made responsible. The liberals of today increasingly identify freedom and liberty with human dignity rather than strictly property rights. . . .

It is often in the public interest to confiscate (and confiscate through majority rule) part of each man's wealth according to how much he can afford, to . . . save . . . the embarrassment of begging in the streets as used to be the common practice. These violations of property rights may be looked upon as desirable from the human standpoint in which the end of society and government is the greatest freedom for all men in the important spheres of life — intellectual and spiritual — or they may be looked upon simply as a good investment propaganda-wise or for the prevention of future revolutions. And these did not come about all at once. They were tried and enacted only after our economic system had broken down, had proven that it was not capable of privately solving the problems. Take, for instance, the example of Minnesota, notably a liberal state in the 1930's. Minnesota did not rush into state relief programs. Governor Floyd B. Olson first set up a committee of 275 to collect money and clothes privately for distribution through established relief centers. The job was handled efficiently and the contributions were generous, but private charity and enterprise proved pitifully inadequate to meet the quantitative and distributive needs of the times. Only after that was a bill introduced to give the government some responsibility for this program through its greater tap of resources and its greater efficiency in distributing help where needed.

Government and politics, economics, history, international affairs, jurisprudence, and the practical political and social issues involved in her field studies made up the most important part of Margaret Weaver's education, and her thinking is rooted in her interest in the law and its requirements. However, the most important educational consequence of her studies lay in the use she made of what she learned in thinking about its implications for all the aspects of life that most occupied her thought. What she learned in the study of the social sciences fed her thinking about theoretical, moral, religious, and educational issues that she also encountered in her studies.

She was a student in a denominational college that required her to take courses in ethics and religion, and here, as in the study of psychology and education, she was faced by the need to see where her ideas about social and political issues, and about the law, led her.

Like a number of the students I talked with, she was, at that point in her life, impressed by the view of man and society she found in Erich Fromm's *The Sane Society.* Half a dozen times in her papers of the last two years in college he is called on to support or illustrate her position. One of her most interesting papers is one presented to her seminar in jurisprudence, in her senior year, which she calls "Our Juridical System: Of Human Bondage." It is a discussion of the differences in the decision-making process in upper and trial courts, and the position of various schools of thought on the subject; but as in all her papers the part that obviously occupied her thought most was the part played in decision making by laws and the part played by men:

> Ever since the dialogue between Plato and Aristotle (and probably before, although not nearly so eloquently or well-preserved), men have been engaged in the great controversy over a government of laws versus a government of men. In our society this is often narrowed to an argument as to whether judges should restrict themselves to the letter law, or whether they should temper this law with judicial discretion. This is, in part, a theoretical question as our judicial system is not structured for a strict law system without the influence of men. Yet, it is valuable for the insights it gives us in tempering and improving our present system as well as its intrinsic interest value.
>
> This paper, while not definitive, will attempt to survey some of the more important and interesting aspects of this last problem. The paper rambles along several paths before it reaches the great garden of truth with a small t, or, in our society, relative conclusions. The paths explored include the pragmatic, practical ways in which a judge may not be completely objective, that is, may interject himself into a case or may not render decisions based purely on the theory of Rule times Fact equals Decision; the various

schools of thought attempting to explain the subjective behavior of judges; and the broader dialogue as to whether the ideal of objectivity or subjectivity ought to reign supreme, or whether either can.

.   .   .   .

Some of the main conclusions that can be traced are: (1) That man is a social animal, judges included, and can, therefore, never completely divorce himself from social and subjective factors; (2) That this is a desirable thing, although not in either extreme of complete objectivity or subjectivity, and the judge is the proper instrument to fill the gap between the static and dynamic in our complex society; and (3) That a realistic concept of law tempered by social justice ought to be recognized and provided for in a trained and aware judiciary, outmoding the elitist concept of natural or fundamental law prevalent before the New Deal and ushering in an awareness of the basic communal, cooperative, and loving nature of man rather than the old concept of a selfish, self-aggrandizing individual.

For support for her view that society must be "ready to recognize the grandeur of human judgment within a compatible system of law . . . a course fraught with dangers and fears" she turns to Fromm:

Fromm's theory is that man is an animal, but transcends this state by being aware of himself. His self-awareness, reason, and imagination disrupt the harmony which characterizes animal existence. Animals are not aware of their being, they live at one with nature, just existing. Man is never free from the dichotomy of his existence — subject to both the animal body longing for "oneness" with nature and with his mind. Reason is man's blessing and his curse, he cannot go back to the harmony of nature, but must make his own world by making the world a human one and becoming human himself — he must proceed to develop his reason.

She quotes *The Sane Society:*

"The fact that man's birth is primarily a negative fact, that of being thrown out of the original oneness with nature, that he cannot return to where he came from, implies that the process of birth is no easy one. Each step into his new human existence is frightening. It always means giving up a secure state, which was relatively known, for one which is new, which one has not yet mastered — the thinking, alive man's task is not to feel secure, but to be able to tolerate insecurity without undue panic and fear. . . . Free man is by necessity insecure; thinking man by necessity uncertain."

Margaret's preoccupation in the paper on "Our Juridical System" was not only a description of its changing nature, but more persistently, the growing recognition of the relative rather than the absolute aspects of justice and truth. She spoke of her effort to arrive at "truth with a small t," and her account of the developing views of the role of the judge and of the law emphasizes the growing importance of socially conditioned factors. She points out that the more we understand the springs of human behavior the more difficult it is to have faith that right solutions can be found just by understanding the law "correctly"; that the great jurists of the twentieth century have cast doubt on the "idea of mechanical jurisprudence wedded to the postulates of an ideal political and economic order" and have demanded a "toleration of uncertainty" as an accompaniment to our greater understanding of the complexities of human nature.

The question of the relativity of values which bothers her in her effort to discuss the problem of government by laws as against government by men shows up again and again in papers throughout her college career. She writes a paper in political philosophy called "Is Natural Law Universal?" in which she discusses conceptions men have held of natural law:

> My conclusion would be that natural law is not universal, if indeed there is such a thing. I am more inclined to the viewpoint that there is no natural law as there is no universal truth. There may be only universal questions.

And the question is explored again in a paper on Burke and Rousseau in which she discusses change as the basis of social organization. In "Some Differences between the Old and the New Liberalism," she writes on de Tocqueville. She quotes Mill's view that "the truth is most commonly found in parts, a little here and a little there" and criticizes de Tocqueville's view that the new democracy is in danger of taking over functions that should be performed by the individual, which is "harmful to the character and the liberty of man by providing him with greater equality through sacrifice of individual initiative." But she points out that he "left room in his doctrines for growth and relativism":

> "Care must therefore be taken not to judge the state of society, which is now coming into existence, by notions derived from a state of society which no longer exists; for as the states are exceedingly different in their structure, they cannot be submitted to a just or fair comparison."

Margaret followed the same road to a view of Christianity, and to an ethical position that she followed in her thinking about law and about government. She wrote a paper on views of Jesus by three "experts," the third being a wry reference to herself and her own effort to think about the nature of Jesus. The two writers she discusses are Rudolph Bultmann, *Kerygma and the Myth,* and Klausner, *Jesus of Nazareth.* From Bultmann she learns the view that "when the mythology is taken away there is still the most important concept left — the redemptive aspect of Jesus's death and resurrection — the judgment of man and the deliverance of man"; Klausner writes of "the historical Jesus, the man. This was Jesus of Nazareth who was afflicted with human frailties, was greatly affected by his environment, and who turned out to be a great teacher of morality and an artist in the use of parables, and who had a lasting influence through the ages."

What she comes to is that "Jesus was no mere visionary or mystic, he was imbued with a sense of practical prudence and was a member of the lower classes, thoroughly immersed in their thinking, toils, and beliefs. He was able to communicate . . . a high moral ethic applicable to the daily life of the people of all classes. . . . [He] was a revolutionary in the full sense of the term. He saw injustices and corruptions in the secular and the spiritual world and he attacked them in no uncertain terms. Jesus was not the gentle, passive, and placable person of Western Christianity."

As a senior she wrote an analysis of determinism, taking her start from a discussion of Whitehead, but finding her principal illustrations, in the end, in the realm of social justice, turning to Clarence Darrrow's explanation of why he "grew to like to defend men and women charged with crime." She quotes Irving Stone's account of Darrow's philosophy:

> "It was at base a philosophy of love and understanding, but to people who did not grasp its implications — that you cannot blame or punish a human machine that has cracked, any more than you can blame or punish a steel machine that has broken down; that you repair it without moral judgment or abuse so that it may carry on with its work — this view seemed fraught with pessimism."

She read Tillich and Huxley and tried to come up with an ethical theory of her own. It would require:

> belief in the order and unity of nature, though it may never be substantiated or wholly discovered, belief in the need of man to tran-

scend and harmonize his own self with the world of matter and outer reality and with the spiritual and moral ideals that have progressively extended themselves in the world. Whether this harmonizing experience is called religion or other terms are used probably makes little difference. There is an ideal of truth which no man will ever find that is applicable to all men . . . as the self he is combining with outer reality, and moral and spiritual value is unique. Therefore, a large degree of tolerance (in the sense of understanding, not indifference) is called for. A scientific method may be used to some extent in at least holding to those values that have been or can be proven to be good or useful though they cannot be proven in the strictest sense . . .

This theory would involve both reason and faith. It would involve tolerance. It would provide for social change and stress its progressiveness and continued extension of its universality. In these respects it is a good moral theory. It has the difficulties of no absolute standards for ethics as ideals — a fault common to all ethical theories. It cannot guarantee that every one would hold the same values or find the same "truth," but it does lend a certain comfort and belief that all who hold this theory would work hard and cooperatively at finding the highest truth and value possible.

. . . .

Tillich says that man is the only animal that finds its existence a problem which must be solved and cannot be escaped. This is man's search for truth in which are found the universal questions — that is, those questions which are always asked in every age — and to which there are no universal answers. Each age will have an answer of its own whether it be found in a god or some other solution.

Postscript, May, 1964

Toward the end of her second year at law school, Margaret wrote:

I am getting along very well. I have learned a great deal in law school about myself, the law, educational philosophies . . . and the ability to think and analyze. I am in my second year and have one left to go. I find the second year rather boring as it consists for the most part of required courses making up the bread and butter diet of most practicing lawyers, such as modern real estate transactions, sales, banking, evidence, trusts and estates, corporations, agency, and tax. Next year will be primarily electives and should be both interesting and challenging.

I have a job for this coming summer and am looking forward to starting. The firm is small, friendly, informal, and liberal. I had quite a time getting the job, however. I hadn't realized the discrimination against women that existed among law firms. . . .

After law school I am planning on practicing with a firm in New

York City provided I can get a job with the firm I want. If that doesn't work out, I may go to Washington, D.C. either with the government or in a political capacity.

.   .   .   .

The paper on taconite . . . is being used as starting research material by a group opposed to the amendment. Needless to say, the last legislature was conservative and succeeded in putting the taconite amendment on the ballot for the coming election. That is another story, and if you are interested, I will tell you about it someday. . . .

The New York Times on May 25, 1964, carried a story about current plans to develop industry in the taconite area of Minnesota, and described steel-industry proposals to establish tremendous plants in the area "contingent on voter approval of the constitutional amendment in November." Thus Margaret's paper becomes a small symbol of what is probably a lost cause, as well as a step in her education.

IV

Public and Private Purposes

BY the time Margaret Weaver had finished college and had had part of a year in law school, becoming a senator was not her only idea about what she might do. Asked how she thought she might function, as a lawyer, in regard to social issues that interested her she said:

> I don't think as a practicing lawyer you do much in a large way, but in a small way — for instance, there are many cases that involve broad social questions, and you can join the issue. But I don't want to do this necessarily. I don't think my future is entirely as a lawyer. There are other things, speaking, writing.

Asked what she would like to do if she were free to choose — what job, in the government, for instance, she would like to have — her response came quickly, "Secretary of Labor."

As her story shows, she came to college with strong political interests; and not only the courses she took, but all the main activities she engaged in during her years there intensified and directed these interests. Scott Hansen, too, in ways different from Margaret — ways determined by the difference in his own nature, his thoughts about his political responsibilities, his lack of Margaret's conviction about a road to travel — was preoccupied most of his time at Harvard with how he should act in a tumultuous world. She was interested in law and the processes of government; he was concerned with how to keep the peace, and how to find a political philosophy by which he might live.

I would like here to comment on the question of students' concerns with public affairs as my interviews revealed them.

The year of these interviews was a year of violence on Southern campuses, of action on the most explosive public issue to involve students in this generation. It was a year of serious efforts to execute the integration order of the Supreme Court, and of hysterical and brutal efforts to prevent it. It was a year of activity for a score of new student organizations on the right and on the left, some interested only in integration or in preventing it, some banding together to protest nuclear testing, some with more general political purposes. In two years they had sprung up almost simultaneously across the country — SPAD, for peace and disarmament; SNCC, the student nonviolent coordinating group of Southern integrationists; the politically liberal Slate, Voice, and Action; and the political right-wing YAF and SAAT. It was as if the students suddenly felt there was something to speak and act for, and tried to find a voice.

In September, 1960, I was on the campus of an unlikely place for student political action — Bennett College, in Greensboro, North Carolina, a college for Negro girls that had no history of political intensity, but rather one of personal gentility. A few months earlier the first sit-in had been staged by four students from the Agricultural and Technical College in that city, and the Bennett students joined at once the movement that spread from it. When the president of the college was urged to take action to prevent this, she quietly said it was a student affair. This was at the beginning of the great wave of sit-ins, basic to integration, and effective beyond the imagination of most people.

It was not the first political activity of these women students. In the presidential campaigns of the year before they had undertaken "Operation Doorknock." Canvassing hundreds of houses to persuade Negro women to register, they served as baby sitters while the women registered, and they succeeded in raising the rolls by scores of names of women who had never registered to vote before.

By 1962 sit-ins had become the great instrument of protest against segregation, and college students, white and Negro, had helped to make it so. In that year, at Spelman College, another important college for Negro women, I talked with a girl who had just been released from thirteen days in an Atlanta jail after a sit-in in which Spelman girls, and boys from nearby Morehouse, had taken part. "It wasn't too bad," she said. "They treated me better than the boys were treated. I was in a large room with about fifty women, who were there for all sorts of reasons, but nobody bothered me."

That week the Spelman student body met at eight o'clock one morning in the auditorium to hear candidates for the presidency of the student council state their platforms, and to hear supporters speak in their behalf. It was a vigorous, outspoken meeting. One of the candidates was a student from Africa, studying in this country for a few years before returning to teach in her own country. The sharpest attack on her candidacy was that as a visitor to this country she would not be able to participate in sit-ins with the rest of the students, and "We can't have a council president who couldn't join a sit-in." And that year, too, fifty of them joined the Peace March in Washington.

It was just ten years after the height of the House Un-American Activities Committee attacks on the colleges — a major force in silencing both students and teachers across the country. During that decade we heard a tremendous lot about the failure of students not only to engage in political activities, but to show any concern with political affairs. It was the decade of the charge of "privatism," of students' preoccupation with their personal well-being, indifference to the public interest.

In 1955 Gillespie and Allport's analysis of the values and expectations of American college students, as compared with students in other lands, reported on "the relatively low interest in social problems. Poverty, delinquency, politics, and race relations are less frequently mentioned in American documents than those of most other lands."* The study included students at Harvard, Radcliffe, and Miami University in Oxford, Ohio, and among these the interest of the Harvard students was lowest. The American student is interested first in a "rich, full life" for himself, and even the higher proportion of Radcliffe students who appear to be interested in public affairs are prompted by the possibility that "social service or education or community work offers the possibility of a career after marriage" and thus contributes to the rich full life the individual wants for herself.

This picture of the American student is repeated many times in the studies of that decade.

The "Class Portrait" of the class of 1957 at Brooklyn College, a detailed study of students who entered in 1953, says "they had not felt impelled to express themselves on controversial issues":

> Their innate sense of responsibility had helped them to develop more mature social attitudes, but had at the same time prevented them from breaking their ties with the world into which they had been born. This feeling of obligation, however, did not extend to the world outside, for the fulfilling of personal aspirations precluded involvement with the community. It is unwise, however, to assume this apparent self-interest was caused by indifference to the needs of others. The ethical standards of life with which they had grown up, had been challenged by their college education, their understanding of human motives had increased, and their insight into social and communal problems had deepened. Just as they had shut their eyes and ears to many intellectual problems, however, they also closed them to the world outside.

* James M. Gillespie and Gordon W. Allport, *Youth's Outlook on the Future,* New York, Doubleday & Company, Inc., 1955, p. 15.

A study for which data were gathered from a number of colleges beginning in 1950, but not published until ten years later, says:

> The investigator attempting to describe the political flavor of contemporary American campuses is immediately and forcefully struck by two themes. The first is what seems to be a remarkable absence of any intense or consuming political beliefs, interests, or convictions on the part of the college student. The second is extreme political and economic conservatism. Both are in marked contrast to the radicalism usually attributed to American college students in the thirties, and said to be a traditional aspect of student cultures in other countries.*

This provides the same picture as Philip Jacob's review of studies of student values, and his own investigation, published in 1956. However, the writers of this study recognize that something had been happening on American campuses between the time they began their investigations and the time they published them. In a footnote they cite the presence on several campuses of new organizations created to combat segregation and compulsory military training:

> As this book goes to press, there seem to be some indications that this trend may be beginning to reverse itself and that perhaps college students' concern about political affairs and public issues may be reviving.†

One sees some clues to what lies behind students' inaction in those years, when they express strong feelings because the causes that captured so many people in the 1930's, for which there were "peace strikes and picket lines on the campuses" fulfilled none of their promises. "Sometimes I feel a little envious, too," a student said, "because they had so much conviction that there was an easy answer. I guess today we know it's much more complicated. Anyway we play it cool."

It is useless to describe the state of political interest among students without reasonable attention to what was happening around them on and off the campus. The investigators of the study just mentioned found a decline of interest on the Cornell campus even between 1950 when they made their first study and 1952 when they repeated it. This was the very height of the McCarthy era. Most of us who were on college campuses at that time know it was the exceptional college or

---

* R. Goldson and others, *What College Students Think,* Princeton, N.J., D. Van Nostrand, Inc., 1960, p. 98.

† Ibid., fn. p. 98.

university that stood firm against the vicious attacks made by the American Legion and other such organizations on educational institutions. Enough has been said of the demoralizing effect of that particular kind of persecution on university faculties from Berkeley to Harvard to raise some question about what we had a right to expect from students.

On the Sarah Lawrence campus, like others the object of particularly violent attacks, membership in the NAACP which had always been prominent on the campus dwindled to almost nothing. But when the NAACP wanted to give a fund-raising party, the students had money in the treasury to pay for the party, and they raised a good deal more. Not knowing this, but knowing only that membership had almost died, the administration offered to subsidize the party. "We don't need it," the students said, "there are enough people who will support the NAACP, but they won't support it with dues and have their names on a membership list. How do we know when that will become a list of subversives?"

Surely any study of political caution among students during those shameful years must recognize causes lying outside the students themselves. There has been no period during our lifetime when the political hopes that gave such lively color to political activity among students during the "radical years" seemed less realistic.

The paralysis of the McCarthy years is passing. Students respond, in political matters, as in other matters, to three pressures — their inner needs, the climate of the college in which they spend four years, and the temper of the times in the world outside the college.

The second and third of these have a large influence on the *form* their effort to deal with their inner, individual needs will take.

The response of students in the past two years to serious and demanding overseas programs, their efforts for desegregation, the political activities, and the partisan magazines — peace strikes and peace walks, the ideologically determined organizations, controversies about speakers of the far right and the far left on campuses — whether it is a conviction of a doom that must be met fighting, or hope that there might be some end to the dislocations, students are speaking again.

It is a time when they are finding encouragement to speak, by the events outside the colleges. Certainly students are being a serious force in desegregation activities, and have made themselves heard on nuclear testing. They have not been following the lead of the majority of adults on either issue because the majority of adults have not declared themselves; but these have become causes into which students can put their feelings and their hopes. The possibility of action that can have meaning, action beyond their private needs, appears almost suddenly to have reality.

The events of the world are providing some use for the belief that there is work to be done beyond the safe confines of personal comfort, and it has not taken students long to know this. The students who have, in the past two or three years of upheaval in this country, added public concerns to their private concerns are probably still greatly in a minority. The adults who have done so are also a minority. But when one adds the hundreds of young people who have entered the Peace Corps to the thousands who have walked in peace marches, anti-discrimination processions, who have picketed and taken part in sit-ins, demonstrated for and against campus speakers on controversial issues, it is fair to guess that concern with public issues among students has risen at a faster pace than among adults.

So much for the world outside the campus. The other force in the lives of college students is the climate of the campus on which they spend their four years. Most studies of indifference report the responses of students to specific questions about their interest in public affairs. We do need this information. But we need also to consider whether the colleges themselves stimulate students' interest in public affairs.

There is no doubt that the crises of the past few years have made many students alert to public issues, with or without the help of the curriculum. If we are interested in the impact of their *formal* education — the teaching in courses, what they study — we need to separate the influences that come from outside the campus, affecting the behavior and beliefs of students, from the influences of individual teachers, and from the design and purposes of the educational program of the college itself.

A report of experience on a campus in the South, where a group of small Baptist colleges for Negro students exist side by side says:

> I found a small group of the alert living side by side with an apathetic majority. The difference seemed to turn on whether they had taken up the challenge of segregation. What I saw of their education made me doubt if it could stimulate even the most determined students.

But the account goes on to speak of "a small group of the intensely articulate and rebellious," and of one of them who sat near the reporter in a pew in the chapel and whispered that:

white students were joining the cause. They seemed to understand the time had come for the end of segregated life.

The central experience for him is the thrill of action with others his age. "You get ideas in jail," he went on; "you talk with other young people you've never seen. Right away we recognize each other. . . . You learn the truth in prison, you learn wholeness. You find out the difference between being dead and alive."*

Even such colleges are serving as places in which students intent on action can find one another, although their education in the courses they study has little or nothing to do with either their purposes or their actions.

Most of the students who discussed their education at length talked about what they looked for in studying, and about their conception of the aims of the college they were attending. In most instances, students found the interest of faculty in promoting concern with public affairs sporadic and occasional — or confined to a small section of the institution. But often these individual efforts of teachers were deeply felt by students; and often they singled out experiences such teachers had provided for them as turning points in their lives.

In larger places, in public universities with a mixed population of students, interest in public affairs, as students reported it, takes several different forms, stimulated in different ways. At Kansas University, situated in a state capital, it was easy to discover an active group of students interested in politics, and using campus activities as a way of becoming introduced to local and state politics. For these it is an extracurricular affair, little related to their studies, and pursued by some of them almost in spite of their education. For some of them it serves as a school for a later political career. Interest in national and international affairs is stimulated for others in the way other special educational experiences are created at that university — by developing special programs for a small group thus separated from the heterogeneous student body. An exchange program with Costa Rica, with a systematic educational life in that country, directed by a member of the university faculty, gives one small group of students an insight into foreign affairs. It is like the honors program mentioned elsewhere, a way of breaking down the large mass of students with heterogeneous interests, into small groups with more cohesive purposes.

In general, however, when students had developed, through their

* Charlotte DeVree, *The Young Negro Rebels,* New York, Harper & Row, 1961.

work, strong convictions about public affairs or an interest in public action, it was almost always under the influence of an individual teacher, and not the result of the curriculum itself or of the atmosphere of the college. At Douglass College the practical and vocational motivation of many students is strong, and professors of political science and economics have found ways of enlarging this motivation by creating opportunities for special studies that raise students' vocational purposes to a sound intellectual level and raise their ideas of possible functions. A program of special studies in political science was designed for a student which allowed her to do field work with the Voice of America. Conferences with the political scientist who directed the project were related to her actual work on it, but involved discussions of political events, interviews and programs involving important national and international issues, wide reading, learning about research methods. She went on to Washington to work as a research assistant and legislative runner on Capitol Hill.

At Brooklyn College there was also, as at Kansas, "extracurricular" interest in political affairs, growing not out of studies in the college, but out of individual interest, except as some professors stimulated this interest or created it, out of their own concerns. Boys went from their studies in labor economics to work in trade unions; a sociologist created for a student opportunity for field work in social planning — a boy who had come to the college from a home where a Socialist father had started his thinking about social issues.

In these places, as I saw them, interest in public affairs was strong to begin with (as in some of the Brooklyn students) or absent to begin with (as with the Douglass students), but in either case was developed by the interest of individual teachers. In neither case was the concern of the institution itself a force developing interest in current public affairs. This is so also in some highly selective private institutions.

A study in one good college reports that about 30 percent of the freshmen thought that, among the purposes of a college education, "to develop one's knowledge and interest in community and world problems" was of "high importance"; at the end of four years of liberal education, only about 34 percent of the same group thought so. Fifty-six percent of the freshmen and 53 percent of the seniors thought it was of "medium importance."

When we remark with dismay the failure of students to be concerned with public issues, it is reasonable to ask what colleges do about it. For these students, at the top of the scale among college students in intelligence, and in potential influence, about two-thirds thought political interest was a matter of medium importance or less in education, and continued to think so throughout their four years. This cannot be entirely a matter of a "naturally" indifferent group of young men; it must bear some relation to the attitudes and values held by their teachers and in some way reflect the content of their education.

The individuals responsible for the curriculum and the intellectual design and atmosphere in most undergraduate colleges would say, if asked, that the education of college students in our time should foster interest in international political issues, in the impact of emerging nations on the world, in issues involving social justice and human rights in this country or elsewhere. They would agree that it should encourage the responsibility of citizens for their immediate community, concern with more education for more people, an effort to deal with the enormous problems and possibilities created by changing technology.

But a serious inquiry into what actually happens in college education cannot rest satisfied with the results of questionnaires addressed to students. It must discover what effort colleges make to develop these interests in students and to encourage responsible action.

What such inquiry should yield is an understanding of the identity or character of the institution itself. Writing of the "multiversity," President Clark Kerr of the University of California says that, when the university began its life it began it as a single community. "It may even be said to have had a soul in the sense of a central animating principle." The modern large American university no longer has this single animating principle, but is a series of communities.

But character, or identity, or "animating principle," is not hard to discover in the case of some colleges which are not so large as to be divided into many souls. Some are identified by original or distinctive academic designs, designs growing out of beliefs about what subject matter and what ways of teaching create a significant education for a student; some are characterized by a moral or social climate, as certain Quaker colleges are; some by their concentration on training students for graduate or professional schools. In many colleges the animating principle is less conspicuous; but in the end, if a college *has* any significant character at all, it is this character, this life-style, that determines the kind of effort it makes to engage the students in their intellectual life.

Some colleges are actively concerned with their students' interest in public affairs and public issues, and stimulate this interest by the design of their curriculum. Some colleges would like to see such interest among the students. Examination of the curriculum and the atmosphere, or life-style, or climate, of the institution would indicate whether or not a college considers developing interest in public affairs a matter to be directly dealt with in educational planning. Many do not.

It is obviously not possible to describe the animating principle of an institution on the basis of interviews with twenty-five students — even students whom one came to know quite well, and who were using the college experience seriously. But it is possible to find some clues.

We have seen that Margaret Weaver came to Macalester College with an interest in political affairs. In a lower-middle-class Republican suburb she emerged from high school one of two Democrats in her school — obviously she had given some high school thought to such matters. She explored many colleges within the range of those available to her, settling on this one because it provided appropriate academic standards and gave opportunity for the kind of study that would advance her interests. We have seen how much latitude and encouragement the college gave her. With her individual experience in mind it might be worth exploring the general environment in which she studied to see how education in this college served the public and private interests of other students.

The students I interviewed in this college differed among themselves a good deal in temperament and many personal qualities, but many of them showed certain common interests, attitudes, and expectations. There is a kind of homogeneity among them which the college recognizes in developing the design of their education. The students I talked with came from modest homes, some from the city, most of them from farms and small towns. Fathers worked for other people — a carpenter, a manager in a mill, a letter carrier. A few were farmers; a few small businessmen.

The college is church-related. Autobiographies the students wrote before they entered the college reveal them as having strong religious feelings — sometimes of a narrow, fundamentalist cast. Religion is central to what many of them say about their ideas about themselves and the possibilities for the future. "I do not know to what work God will call me, but that he will call me I feel sure" — the statement is somewhat extreme but the view is one often expressed in the high-school-age autobiographies of the students I interviewed when they were college juniors or seniors.

The most obvious effect of the education this college gave such students was to channel their sense of mission into fields of social and political concern and action. An interest in international affairs stamped the life of the college and the activities of many of its best students. The college encouraged foreign students. There was much talk about the Peace Corps, and every year the college had a week-long series of conferences on political issues that was spontaneously mentioned by many students as a spur to their interest in political affairs.

Eight or nine Minnesota colleges participate in a foreign-study program called SPAN. A number of these students were part of that project, which is knit into their regular academic work. Students from the various colleges involved meet in seminars for a year, preparing by study and discussion for the summer of work abroad. On their return they prepare a paper, and the project becomes part of their academic record. Some illustration of this experience is given later (pp. 167–168).

Most of the students said they thought the liveliest and most interested students major in the social sciences, and they found the reason for this in the encouragement the college gave by these programs, and in the presence of one or two teachers who seem to have provided important intellectual experiences. Of one of these teachers a student said:

> The most important thing I learned from him was that we should not expect to get rid of political conflict — that conflict was in the nature of the associations of men; that what we had to do was to try to make better decisions rather than worse ones every time we had a decision to make. This has been important to me in thinking about all sorts of things besides politics.

A student from Tanganyika wrote, in the college paper, the week after his country declared its independence, his story of its emergence as a nation, and in the course of it said:

> I am privileged that I have Dr. X, the professor of political science, to work with. Through him I have learned that if there were such a thing as "peaceful transference of power," there would be no need to study political science.

The students I talked with are intelligent; only one is particularly gifted. They are serious and modest, have a sense of worth, and objectives for their lives that engage them with other people. A number of the boys were headed for law school. One of the professors explained the comparatively large number:

> A number of these students would make very good college teachers, and perhaps some of them will end up in academic life.

But the goal is too far away for most of them. They come from homes not accustomed to the idea of long professional preparation; and they not only don't have the funds for it, but they can't be financially dependent on families or even on fellowships for that long. They need to be successful, if they are to justify their college years, and going to graduate school for the years needed for the Ph.D., spending more years as low-salaried instructors, moving slowly through an assistant professorship, until they finally come out, having been productive enough scholars to warrant it, to an associate professorship and some financial security and, especially, some professional prestige — it's too long for most of them to wait. The law is much faster — three years after they leave here they are ready to embark on a respectable professional career. It is something tangible they and their families ask.

As young lawyers, such students have had successful experiences with men in political life and in government service. They become assistants to legislators and to representatives in Washington. "Minnesota is a politically minded state," one of them reminded me, and he added that in the college the sense of political responsibility was strong, and was encouraged in such students.

Margaret Weaver's story illustrates one kind of motivation we find among these students. The experience of William Rogers, another student, illustrates a way many of the students find direction.

He entered college intending to major in psychology and go into the ministry. This was, indeed, the justification, in his family's eyes, for his going to college at all. He was active in church work before coming to college, and he chose this college because it was a church-related institution. His family had a small farm which gave them a modest livelihood, but they were unable to help him financially. By the time he reached his senior year he knew he did not want to become a minister; his interest and attention had turned to political science, although the pressure from home to keep to the original plan was strong. Like others, as he became interested in political science he began to plan for law school as preliminary to entering politics; but the next shift was made when he decided not to go into law, but to go to graduate school and into college teaching and, he hoped, later into politics. He talked about his interest and the interest of other boys from rural, conservative, religious backgrounds in politics, and said he thought it usually started from their knowledge of the problems of people they knew, and of the needs of the farming sections of the state.

His religious upbringing was an important force in the development of his intellectual concerns:

> The course in political philosophy was a turning point for me. It helped me to arrange what I learned in history. It gave me a conceptual base for my Calvinist-Presbyterian upbringing.

And the influence of the college on the students' religious beliefs parallels its influence on their political and social views:

> You tend to change the way you believe, here, but not what you believe. The course in Old Testament history makes a strong impression — it does on most of us. It is a broadening course; but it tends, too, to destroy the faith of some students who feel that if they can't believe in a literal interpretation of the Bible they can't believe at all. But it can strengthen your belief — as you study other things, learn, learn to think and to ask questions. People who have never even thought to ask questions begin to take the Bible no longer with the blind faith they had been used to. But speculation gives a firmer base on which to stand, which might have been lost altogether without this kind of study.

A political science professor who works with many such students describes them as first-generation boys, upward mobile, ambitious, who have a sense of mission, who must accomplish. They can get here a direction and a discipline that will let them go on and let them function. They achieve important places for young men — one is secretary to an important legislative committee, one became an assistant to Senator Humphrey, they are in political offices where they can learn and can be effective.

It seems obvious that the interest such students as these have in political life is affected by the way the college directs their education, recognizing and building on the motivations they come with. And it is obvious, too, that to understand low or negative evidence of public purposes among students we need to know what the institution does about encouraging or not encouraging these interests.

V

Alex Rovere at The New College, Hofstra

MARGARET WEAVER came to college positively convinced of her destiny — that is, she had in mind what she wanted to be and do; Scott Hansen came, one might say, negatively convinced — that is, he was good at mathematics and saw no reason for not going into mathematics.

As time went on, Margaret's interests and purposes remained clear, but the exact road she would travel was open when she graduated. She is studying law; she thinks she will probably not simply practice law; she is interested in and expects to work on matters relating to government, legislation, politics — but just *how* remains to be seen. Scott Hansen came to understand himself better, to discover and explore values and beliefs, and to recognize his need for more knowledge to deal with issues he had discovered to be important. He may teach, since teaching gives a man a chance to continue to acquire knowledge and to explore — by himself, with like-minded colleagues, and with students — questions that concern him. But just where this search for knowledge will lead him he does not surely know.

No student I talked with entered college with less conviction about what he should do with his life or his education than Alex Rovere, and none ended more single-minded or more certain where he wanted to go. Four months before he finished college, ready for graduate work in science, he knew that he wanted to do research at the borderline where physics, chemistry, and biology meet. His only uncertainty was whether he would be allowed to study where he wanted to study, and whether he would be good enough intellectually.

The recent national sense of urgency about developing scientists has led many people in the past ten years to inquire into the making of scientists — who are they, where do they come from, what are their personal and intellectual characteristics, their backgrounds. The research tells us that a high school student who wins a Westinghouse Talent Search award is likely to be the first-born son of an educated, urban, professional family with above-average income. The family has a permissive, democratic attitude toward the young man. In school he had friends with whom he shared his scientific interests, and he knew and imitated scientists. Other studies describe the background of scientists in about the same way — they tend to come from families of adequate means who emphasize learning and the intellectual aspects of life. Frequently they are first-born children. Sixty percent of the eminent scientists studied by Anne Roe in *The Making of a Scientist* fit this picture.

The studies speak of the early commitment to science: "Some educators now believe that between 60 and 70 percent of those now getting advanced degrees in science made their vocational choices before entering colleges." The influence of other boys and girls on the development of a firm wish to study science is also often mentioned as a significant factor — the prospective scientist as a boy in school finds and consorts with friends who have curiosity about the same things he is curious about. They reinforce each other's interest. A popular picture of a scientist makes him out a queer sort of fellow, and he tends to seek and find those who speak the language he is trying to speak. The size of the community in which one grows up is apparently important — "a large percentage of eminent American scientists were raised on farms or in small villages." And of course the potential scientist has high test scores and a good school record.

Alex Rovere fits not a single one of these criteria. One way in which he *does* fit the picture is that he was not educated in a conspicuous or "prestige" institution. Like many other studies, the Knapp and Goodrich *Origin of American Scientists* speaks of the high percentage of eminent scientists who come from small, sometimes obscure, liberal arts colleges.

One is inclined to think that — in the matter of background, family, early schooling, early interests, school grades, and everything else — Alex is so far from the "normal" science student that his history itself will enlighten us little about anything except Alex Rovere. But his history raises questions about both the scientific and the non-scientific education of a student who wants to be a scientist; and indeed about the education of those who began by thinking they wanted to be scientists and changed their minds. It is worth considering on those grounds. Moreover, whenever one penetrates below the surface experience of students in all sorts of colleges, one can expect to find that most of them, however apparently "typical," reveal individuality that makes sport of the image of what *is* typical.

Alex Rovere has a lot to say about what it was like studying science in high school; what he thinks made it possible for him to make a "creative leap" in college; his own attitude toward himself as a person, and to scientists as persons; what he has come to believe being a scientist will do for his knowledge, for man's knowledge in general, and for the use he might be in the world and to other people. And he has a lot to say about other aspects of his education at college — he tells us where literature, history, politics stand in his scale of significance.

All these issues enter into the speculation about a scientist's education. They have engaged the attention of many people concerned about the creation of scientists, and also about how to teach science to people who will not be scientists. How, they ask, can we utilize this exploding body of knowledge in education? And for whom can we use it? Since about 1952 exhaustive research on these questions has been carried on.

Almost every student I spoke with, science major or not, talked about his experience with science, as a student. This talk, against the background of research on education in science, tells another side of the story — not the one we learn from Alex Rovere. This other side is found in the chapter entitled "In and Out of Science," which follows his story.

There are two parts to the story of Alex's response to his education — what studying science came to mean to him, and what studying other things meant. The first part of his story is the account of an intense, single-minded, intellectually ambitious commitment to the study of science, and of a faith that scientific knowledge comes nearer to the heart of what is important in life than any other knowledge. The second part tells of an almost complete unwillingness to allow any other study to become important, or even to explore the possibility that it might help his intellectual growth.

Because of this single-mindedness, he does not have a liberal undergraduate education. The college faculty included men and women who interested themselves greatly in this boy's growth — and were able to give him an entirely new view of what science is. He took the courses appropriate to a liberal education. But his education failed to develop in him any interest in humanistic studies, or any conviction that they were important to his intellectual or personal life, and it is easy to make the judgment that it thus failed him in a serious way.

But Alex's education posed a special problem: it was only when he arrived at college that he was born into the world of scientific inquiry. Not only did he lack the vision of himself as a scientist that the Westinghouse and the National Merit Scholarship students bring with them from high school; he lacked even the most rudimentary knowledge of the very branches of science that were to become immensely important to him in the few years at college.

He said in his application form that he had liked biology best in high school, and his grade in biology was higher than any other grade in his whole high school course. But that was in his freshman year in high school; and his grades in physics and chemistry, in his second and third years, ranged from 72 to 58. When, in college, he "discovered" science he devoted himself to it unremittingly. Apparently all his other studies were a matter of going through motions. He spent on them as little time as he could manage. "I've a Latin exam this afternoon," he said one day, "I won't do very well. I put the time into it I had to, to cover the assignments, but not the extra time I would have needed to get a good grade — I didn't have it to give." In response to the comment that in this respect he was in the same position as the other students, he said, "Oh, but I'm not. Look at the other fellows in the physics and mathematics classes — they began way down in the ninth grade learning things I have had to learn in a hurry now. They are years ahead of me; I'll be years catching up. I haven't time."

One wonders what it would have taken to convey to this determined boy the idea that it might be important to study literature or history or government or art; whether this incomplete, one-sided education was all he *could* absorb at this point. He was willing to discuss these matters at length. Since his relation to the study of science is so sharply divided from his interest in studying anything else, I have told his story in terms of what he thought about science, and then what he thought about the things he encountered that were not science.

"The Worse It Got, the More Time I Spent on Other Things"

Nobody in my family had gone to college — they liked the idea that I might become a doctor.

WHEN he entered college Alex Rovere listed medicine, medical research, and psychology, in that order, as possible occupations. He said he liked to build model boats and airplanes, work on cars, fish, play football, and read. He was for four years president of his class at the small and rather poor Catholic school he came from, and was on the debating team. He took part in dramatics and served on the dance committee of the school. He worked during the last two years of high school as an apprentice carpenter, earning $50 a week, and he worked to pay his way through college.

His grades in high school declined quite steadily from the first year to the fourth — 90 the first year in religion and 77 the fourth; 83 in freshman mathematics and 72 in his junior year; 93 in freshman biology, 58 in chemistry two years later; 97 in first-year Latin and 70 in fourth-year Latin. It was clear that his interest and attention steadily waned and he ended by failing a course in physics, repeating it in the summer session and failing it again.

"The worse it got," he said, "the more time I spent on other things" — as president of his class, on extracurricular activities. This increase of extracurricular activity as a consequence (rather than a cause) of lack of academic success was mentioned by a number of other students, too.

When he failed physics the second time he got into a jeep with a friend and they headed west without telling anybody where they were going — "I ran away from home; I didn't know what else to do." His family caught up with him in Chicago and brought him back.

He had gone to a parochial school where, he said, the teaching was very bad. His account of the school was not hostile — he said he thinks the brothers did as well as they could, but they were poorly educated and could not teach the things they were supposed to teach. "The chemistry teacher didn't know any chemistry, but somebody had to teach it, so he did." He is, however, indignant at the control the school exercised on what was taught — he pronounced it "shameful" to have to study biology in the terms in which these teachers have to teach it. Asked if he was a Catholic, "I *was* a Catholic," he replied, and that was the only time he ever mentioned it.

Looking back after two years of successful experience with the study of science in college he says he is astonished at the way science was taught in the high school — not only his school, he says, but schools his friends went to, too. "The whole school was geared to pass the Regents' examination — that is what the curriculum was" in his school. In science there was never discussion of theory; you memorized certain problems and nobody ever undertook to discuss anything that was involved in the processes you went through in getting the answers to the problem. "You put down the formula and plugged in the numbers."

Talking about himself as he was before he came to New College he said that the college had made an immense difference in his total life:

My family was very poor, and we lived in a very poor district —
I don't know whether it was a slum or not, but it was nearly a slum,
anyhow. I remember looking around me to find out who the *men*
were, and they seemed to me to be the athletes. I got interested in
the boxers and went around to the boxing clubs a good deal. They
seemed very masculine to me, and I imitated the way they talked
and the way they walked. I was good at athletics, and got good at
boxing, and thought I might become a boxer, because that seemed
a pretty good thing around there. Then I got up here, and I discovered you could be a man without talking bad English — that it
wasn't sissy.

"I Don't Know Why They Let Me In"

ALEX ROVERE came into The New College with the first class of students. The New College was started in the fall of 1959 as a separate, but
related, unit of Hofstra University. The term "experimental" used to
describe an educational institution is just now more suspect than it has
been at some times in the past, and if one wished to be suspicious this
new college would provide ample grounds. It is necessary to say something about the institution in describing what happened to Alex Rovere
when he entered it.

The New College was organized particularly for the purpose of de-
signing a freshman year that would "offer the freshman an intellectually
challenging and cohesive year."

It was not an "honors college," nor a branch of Hofstra University
for gifted students; the designers of the program intended the students
to be as nearly like the students in the parent college as possible.

For several reasons this could not quite happen. Special motives
induce students to enter a new and experimental college. These motives
are mixed and varied, but they lead to a self-selection process that will
make the students differ in subtle if not observable ways from those in
the original college. Three kinds of students can be identified in such institutions — they can be found in Monteith College of Wayne University, also an experimental program with a very different curriculum
from that in the parent college; it was possible to identify them at Sarah
Lawrence College from the first. There are some who think the demands of a new institution (especially one that publicly indicates more
flexibility in the program than is customary) might be easier to meet. A
number of the Monteith students interviewed were clear that this
prompted them to come — although it was not what prompted them to
stay. And New College students confirmed this. Some wanted to come

to college, or had ulterior motives for coming to college, but disliked the academic life generally, and hoped they might escape from its most undesirable aspects in the new institution. Some were genuinely adventurous and inquiring people who were captivated by the chance to work in what promised to be an exciting environment.

In some instances students think it is easier to get into a new and untried institution than into an established one, but in this instance it was decided that a student should have a record that would admit him to Hofstra University before he could be given an opportunity to enroll in The New College.There are unknowns in this process, too. Whether, without a New College as a possibility, Alex Rovere would have been accepted at Hofstra, we cannot tell. One wonders whether the interested and adventuresome Fellows who were to be the faculty of The New College, and who interviewed prospective students, would have recommended altogether the same group (including Alex) if the students were all to have become regular Hofstra freshmen — whether, that is, the faculty members were perhaps interested in taking some gambling chances on the power of their new program.

Hofstra University is a suburban commuting university on Long Island and has had as its general standard the admission of students described as "good average students," in terms of College Board scores. It has, of course, many who are much better than that; but it was such students who were expected to form the main part of the student body of The New College. The first two classes of The New College had a mean verbal score on the aptitude tests of about 575 and a mean mathematics score of about 560. The selection of students for the third class was made on a somewhat different basis from the selection of the first two years, and the mean scores for that year rose to 600 and 585.

But in a year when the verbal score was about 575, and the mathematics score about 560, Alex Rovere was admitted with a verbal score of 448 and a mathematical score of 513. On all visible grounds he was an unpromising student, and he would have had difficulty being admitted to college under ordinary circumstances. These first applicants were interviewed with some care, however, and somebody decided this boy had promise justifying his admission to the new institution, with its new and perhaps startling program which was a drastic departure from what any of the students had known in high school. Moreover it was staffed by a faculty interested in and confident of the program, most of whom had participated in its creation, all of whom had excellent reputations as teachers, all of whom had confidence in students and took pleasure in teaching them.

These faculty members, called Fellows, taught only at The New College — no faculty member or student belonged partly to Hofstra and partly to New College. A provost was the educational head of the new institution, and its only administrative officer. All official records were handled in the regular registrar's office. The six faculty members worked closely with the students, and, as the program was arranged, came to know all the students in this group; indeed, all faculty participated in teaching the one course that was required for all students. Educational decisions were made by the faculty, who constituted together, as one person put it, the curriculum committee for The New College. Changes, judgments, errors, satisfactions and dissatisfactions with the teaching, the content, the quality of the students' work were within the exclusive experience and power of the six faculty members — and it was their college in a way that few colleges are the possession of their faculty in these years of crowded institutional life. Students from the very beginning had the experience of a variety of learning processes: lectures, seminars, discussion groups, and independent study. Student-faculty relationships were close, and students had the advantage of frequent individual conferences.

This was the college to which Alex Rovere came, with an unenviable high school record behind him, no study habits, and the idea that it would be a good thing to be a doctor. For one thing, undertaking to say he would be a doctor gave him the only excuse for going to college, he thought, that would carry weight with a family not much interested in education. "It's a status symbol to them — and I guess the white coat had some glamor for me, too." Up to the time he entered New College the male figures he looked up to were the athletes at the boxing club. He is still not clear about why he wanted to go to college except that he had no better alternative.

He was anxious enough to ask, in reply to the letter admitting him to The New College, for the name of a chemistry book that might help him prepare for his first year in college, and he was given the name of the text to be used.

The main thing that happened to Alex Rovere when he came to New College is that he met Professor Adolph Anderson, a teacher who had left an important post in an important college to undertake the exacting and uncertain task of introducing a mixed, middle-level, scientifically uncommitted group of a hundred students to the idea of scientific evidence and the ways of scientific behavior; and to teach chemistry to a small group similarly mixed but probably with more motivation for the study of chemistry.

Although Hans Rosenhaupt wrote of a different kind of student at a different level of development in a piece called "Gimlet Eye and Fatherly Hand," what he says has as much meaning for a college freshman like Alex Rovere as it does for the graduate student the writer has in mind. It says something of what Alex found:

> The contemporary student's quest for a teacher at the other end of the log bears a striking similarity to the nightmarish search of the hero called K in Franz Kafka's *Castle*.
>
> The intellectual has recently been enjoined to build his house separate from the world around it, and to waste as little time as possible on such desultory activities as loving the other occupants. I, an educational romantic, find comfort in discovering an occasional graduate department resembling the Cavendish Laboratory in Cambridge at the height of its glory, when Rutherford stomped through its halls singing Onward Christian Soldiers. It is, incidentally, no accident that the close master-disciple relationship has been preserved among natural scientists. The physical nearness of master and pupil, the daily contacts in the laboratory, the relative abundance of faculty, and, most important, an atmosphere of being engaged in a common enterprise — all these factors combine to preserve in the science sector of graduate education the master-disciple relation.*

Certainly the fatherly hand was needed; but the fatherly hand alone could not make it possible for this unprepared boy to get an education without the gimlet eye, which was there. He said "Professor Anderson did everything for me."

"What was the most important thing he did for you?"

"He taught me to think."

"What does that mean? — it is so easy to say."

"Thinking — how to take one step at a time to find out what you want to know — the wonderful experience of being able to do that. He didn't answer questions; he said, 'What are the alternatives?' But he helped you along — 'Now let me say this alternative won't do. Why not?' And he got you to work on every possibility, one after another. What is important about chemistry is what it shows about how the physical universe is made and what all this means in terms of human life."

* *The Graduate Journal*, Vol. V, No. 1, Spring 1962.

This conversation took place in his second year, when he had gone on to Hofstra and was also back at The New College serving as assistant to Anderson with the new crop of beginning students. But even the first year the "problem sessions" and the small discussion groups which met from time to time to work on problems together or to discuss reading or a lecture, both gave Alex the chance and faced him with the necessity to learn, to struggle with ideas or problems, and to communicate with other students. A recording of a problem session he conducted shows the effort he was making to accomplish this, even in that freshman year.

Faculty members interviewed Alex at the beginning of the year and decided that, despite the physics fiasco, he should take, as his specialized afternoon course, the chemistry course taught by Mr. Anderson; if he had any thin thread of motivation, it was toward the study of medicine. It was here that he began to learn, as he put it, "what chemistry is."

About Christmas time, that first year, perhaps three and a half months after he began studying in the new program, he came in to see Mr. Anderson. He said, "What I have to know now is whether you think I have what it takes to go into medicine. I have to make up my mind now, because this is my last chance to get into the Golden Gloves competition."

That afternoon he gave up boxing — a kind of certificate of commitment to try to study.

By the end of the first year he had abandoned the idea that he would be a doctor, and decided he wanted to be a theoretical chemist:

> I don't want to do the experiments in the lab. It was the lab that first made me see what chemistry is — that and Mr. Anderson's talk — and how one *can* think about it — it was there I began to work out the alternatives — but I don't need that now.

Several important things happened to him that first year. The "morning course," as it was called, officially began with one week of discussion of writing by the literature teacher and a series of short papers by the students which were discussed during the sessions of that week. There was no separate writing course, but writing, in relation to everything the students studied, was important, and continual, and papers were carefully read and discussed with them. During the first half of the year they wrote about sixteen essays; during the second half of the year they wrote six large essays requiring research and proper presentation. Students could not complete the credits for the year unless their writing reached a satisfactory level. Students needing special help received it until they could work on their own.

As a senior Alex recalled most often the expanding study of science that first year, and the time he spent working at writing:

> The main thing about Mr. Acres was perhaps an introduction to a lesson in how to read. And this, of course, is important. To get back to science: I feel that many students can't — they don't know how to read, and they don't know how to *understand* what is being presented to them. But Mr. Acres tried to teach us how to read. He also tried to teach us how to express ideas — our ideas — and he showed us — particularly myself — that what I *wrote* was not what I *thought*. You see, I just couldn't *put down* what I wanted to say — just think of yourself, you've had a couple of years of college, and you can't say what you want to say. How ridiculous this is, and what are you accomplishing? And this was a tremendous aid. I found that I could write, I can be an average writer, but it takes me time. "Is this what I want to say?" In other words, it takes my time. I don't find it as easy as explaining a theory to somebody.

"What Is This Problem Asking Me?"

> When I came to college from high school all I was able to do was memorize. You can differentiate between just letting your passions overrule you, or sitting down and being able to reason. All I was able to do was just to memorize. . . . I was never able to understand mathematics, and I failed . . . particularly advanced algebra and trigonometry. I had an awful lot of trouble with it and when I came to chemistry I just barely passed it with a 67. Then I came to New College and I found that I had to take general chemistry as a required course for medical school. I was afraid to take this course, I really was, and when I started it I found it very difficult; and as I sat in class I thought everybody else knew what was going on because they were all so quick in raising their hands, and I was so lost. I used to go home and put in hours and hours and it just couldn't sink in.
>
> What was worse was that Dr. Anderson used to single me out and make me go to the blackboard and say, "Well, be specific, now; explain what you are trying to do." And I was terribly embarrassed all the time, and I began to resent him for this. And he kept it up all semester long. But as it turned out, toward the end of the first semester I began to understand what chemistry was like, and how you have to think in order to master the subject; I ended up among the top four in the class.

He tried to explain what he meant by saying he began to understand what chemistry was like:

> Well, the biggest thing is, if you have a problem, or there's a definition, try and ask yourself, "What is this problem asking me; what are they giving me, and how can I tie the thing together?" Or, if it's a definition, "What is the definition telling me, do I understand this, can I put it into my own words and make it fit in with the type of thinking you have to do in chemistry?" This is what I realized; not just taking a definition down and memorizing it, and being able to come up with an answer — this is of no value, because if a person comes in with a slight trick in the problem, then you're lost; but in the beginning that was all I was able to do.

He found the second semester more difficult:

> It is considered more difficult, and that's because the ideas are more abstract, and you get closer to basic ideas. Dr. Anderson kept coaxing me into forgetting how to memorize and just learn how to think. It wasn't important if I remembered specific things; but it was important if I understood what was going on; and this is the way I began to try to work. Going home, in the afternoon, I forgot about memorizing. I used to read the book and ask myself over and over, "Do I understand it?" I used to close the book and make pictures in my mind and I found after that that I had no trouble. Once I felt that I could do the work I used to say to myself, "Come on, let's go, and see if you can get ahead." And I used to go to the laboratory, and they gave me all the free time I needed and all the equipment I needed, and I carried on extra experiments. And when I saw myself the laws that we have in chemistry being displayed by nature, my interest started to grow. I decided to be a chemistry major.

Alex finished that first year at The New College and entered Hofstra:

> I had to face the second challenge, which was mathematics. Pure mathematics is the most advanced of the sciences. It's a more abstract subject than chemistry; and I find that it just requires a great deal of horse sense. You just have to sit down and try to —— oh it's so difficult to say —— it's the downfall of so many students. What I'm trying to say is if you see a big equation, or a complicated diagram in geometry, don't panic, because the author of the textbook, or the pioneers in mathematics, were not trying to develop a subject that was supposed to be a mystery, and everybody supposed to be afraid of this thing. That wasn't their idea.

For all the brave intentions, advanced algebra, which he took in the summer session immediately following that first long year at The

New College "was very disappointing to me. I got a D in summer school — perhaps it was too fast. I don't know what it was." He was working to support himself at the same time, and perhaps that had something to do with it, too.

He repeated the mathematics in the fall semester and "had no trouble at all — I did very well in the course. In fact, I wound up helping people in my class." He was finally able to put what he had learned about studying from Mr. Acres and Mr. Anderson to work in the service of mathematics:

> It was my first breakthrough in mathematics. I finally felt I was getting something; finally developing the kind of mind it takes to understand these mathematical ideas. The second semester was calculus. I was always afraid of calculus because everybody — I used to see — like I said before, these complex equations and I said, "Oh my God I'll never be able to understand this." But I did very well in calculus; just by sitting down, not trying to memorize — just trying to think. When the first semester of calculus was over I found myself completely amazed, by all the powerful — by all the *tools* of calculus — how powerful the subject was — how many things we could do. Such as taking the area of complex curves — it's so easy in calculus and I realized how significant this tool was, and how important it was in the development of physics and chemistry.

The fall of the second year when he was studying at Hofstra, he was made assistant in the general chemistry course he had taken the previous year at New College. He was an eager and interested teacher. He found working with students a spur, and the relationship with Dr. Anderson continued. It was obvious that in those first two years the Fellows, New College, and especially Dr. Anderson, were his models. He described how he dealt with the freshmen in the chemistry class — it was a repetition of what he had gone through with Anderson the year before:

> When they ask me a question I say "What don't you understand?" And when they say, "I don't know," I say, "Open the book and read his definition to me"; and I make them read it very slowly, and I make them repeat it in their own words, and eventually they see how easy it is. That's what I feel; the beauty of science is that some one great man contributed this thing to the world. His initial contribution was very difficult, but the beauty of it is that after that, everybody can understand it. Einstein made his theory of relativity understood by anybody. In fact, he enjoyed talking to people of non-science interests.

He talked about what the creators of the calculus had achieved for later scientists:

> Newton was trying to explain planetary motion; the cofounder, Leibnitz, was not concerned with physical implications. But it is his calculus we use today in physics and chemistry. I think calculus is a pure part of mathematics. In other words, when these men devised this it was of no importance to them whether it was applied or not. They were just trying to master certain ideas which were extremely difficult to the Greeks. Newton himself said he was not great, just a midget standing on the shoulder of a giant. But today calculus, differential equations, is a means for making the expressions of the theories which we devise in physics or chemistry reproducible. I think we could have physics, but a physics textbook would be ten times as big as it is today without calculus, without differential equations. Mathematics is an art in a sense that it takes creative ability to devise this. We are not looking at any phenomenon of nature, like physics or chemistry, where we perform an experiment and try to get what we want out of it. In mathematics it is different. We have no place to seek an answer to our questions. We just sit down and try to explain it with our knowledge in the past of mathematics. Mathematics being an art is used as a tool in chemistry and physics, as I said, to make things reproducible in an easier way. These subjects could exist without mathematics — much more difficult though.

From Medicine, to Chemistry, to Research in Physical Chemistry

By the end of his first year, Alex had abandoned the idea that he would be a doctor, and decided he wanted to be a chemist. It was an intensive and concentrated program he followed after his freshman year. He was admitted to a special course in radiobiology, and throughout the turns and changes in his thinking about what he should do, and in the courses he selected, he had the double task of studying the fundamental mathematics and science he started learning late, and discovering what field of science he was to follow. During this second year his ideas began to expand; and he commenced to learn something about the relations of physics, chemistry, and biology.

In the second semester of his second year he took a course in nuclear physics. Both advanced calculus and elementary physics were prerequisites to this course, and he had studied neither.

> But I felt it was a challenge for me and I wanted to do it. I asked permission of the physics department and they said, if you think

you can pass, go ahead and try. This is the course that opened up my mind, or has brought me to where I am now. In studying nuclear physics I realized that in order to explain the phenomena we encounter in chemistry it is difficult to separate chemistry from physics. As I said, physics is the most advanced of the sciences outside of pure mathematics. Chemistry is directly dependent upon physics for the understanding of atomic and molecular structure. Ultimately all the questions of chemistry lead to this. Biological chemistry, no matter what, they all come down to atomic and molecular structure. Chemistry is dependent upon physics. I realized this from nuclear physics.

Without having had the calculus I realized I was at a disadvantage because the other students had had advanced calculus as a matter of fact. But for the topics which I had not had I went to the library and took out a book and explained it to myself and found it worked very well. I did well in the course and I scored higher than others who had had advanced calculus.

"How much did you have to do on your own?" I asked.

Quite a bit, quite a bit, oh quite a bit. And I was working at the same time and that made it hard.

But you have no idea that when you realize how basic something is to the understanding of a complex subject like chemistry, it just gives you such a tremendous drive that you don't realize the time that's going by. One or two o'clock in the morning. It's not that it's work — you don't realize that it's work — it's just sheer enjoyment. I never thought I would be able to think along these lines. I realize you don't have to be a genius to try to be a good scientist. You have to have a basic understanding of your subject and be interested in working, and that is what it takes.

In a way this thinking began in the first year, when what was involved in the study of medicine began to take on reality for him — began to be something more than an image of a man in a white coat:

Let me say why I decided to leave medicine. I tried to think of what it takes to be successful in medical school, and what it takes to be successful in graduate study in science, and I came up with the conclusion that they are two different types of disciplines. Medicine is a tough grind — but I don't think it is as intellectually challenging as graduate school. The type of learning is different. In medical school you are required to memorize certain things; in graduate school studying science will be different. I think it requires an understanding and an ability to think and reason about what is put before you. In medical school, for instance, in the first year you take a course like gross anatomy and all you have to do is memorize. I see no point in doing this. The reason I don't see any point is because my interests do not lie in amassing all these facts, but in trying to explain why these things come about. I don't look down on medicine; I know how important it is. But they teach you to be a healer, they do not teach you to be a scientist. . . . Chemistry and physics are more basic to understanding the universe than medicine will ever be.

Having turned to chemistry, he as quickly ruled out some aspects of that field:

I realize that there are fields in chemistry which are not dependent on physics, such as synthetics, fibres — all that; and that men can work in these fields who have no interest in why the thing works — just to produce a product, and if it works and makes money for the company, fine. I can't do that.

By the time he was thinking concretely about graduate school he had found the direction he wanted to go:

I have made up my mind to go to graduate school to study physical chemistry. I have to master the basic concepts of chemistry, physics, and mathematics — it is the only way I can enter the discipline of physical chemistry.

He began to consolidate his ideas about what he wanted from the study of science, and two important things emerged — he wanted to do research in a field that called on knowledge of chemistry, physics, and biology; it should be research that made a direct contribution both to knowledge and immediately to human welfare:

About biology — today people say you don't need math for biology. That is a misconception. Biology and medicine I feel are the most difficult because biology is dependent upon chemistry which is in turn dependent upon physics, and you must have a mastery of mathematics to work in these fields. A person who is in the biological sciences and the medical sciences should really have a complete understanding of chemistry, mathematics, and physics, and it is a rare occasion to find somebody like this, and I feel this is one reason why our progress has been so slow in the medical sciences — that perhaps they're not attacking the problem the right way.

The other important thing that emerged was his discovery of Linus Pauling, and such a hero to worship intensified the flame that had already been lit:

Linus Pauling is now working at Caltech on mental disease, using the methods of this science. I don't know about his work, but he is working at the molecular basis of mental disease. He believes as we understand more about the molecular structure of the body we need to begin to explore how the mind works, and what physical basis we can find for mental disorders. I went to the Atlantic City meetings of the Chemical Society, and it was the opinion of most of the men down there that if he lives long enough he would solve this problem.

Alex had grown into a good deal of self-confidence by the time his plans for himself began to crystallize. He took pleasure in tutoring, in testing himself by tutoring in subjects he had not regularly studied, but had worked at on his own. "Mostly it isn't for pay — I like being able to do it." But he apparently struggled a good deal about what, in the end, he would be able to do:

> I try to ask myself, would I be more use in medicine than I could be in science. The chance of doing something significant in science is extremely small. It takes a lot of luck — you can't describe it as luck. Take the gifts Einstein, Rutherford, and all those men have contributed. In medicine at least as a physician I could help people out. I could every day help at least one person — I would be bound to do something useful. But I don't know if I will have this chance in science. I thought besides research I could teach, and perhaps if I couldn't do something significant some person I taught would do something significant.

But in spite of the doubts, he had already begun to get the feel of research, and it became clearer as the months went on that the wish to do research would have to be satisfied.

In his senior year he undertook to do research on the mechanism of coordination of a compound of serium and water. He said, in the course of that year, that he had not expected to do anything significant in this research:

> The reason I took it was to try to get an understanding of what research was like and it's been very helpful — I'm glad I did it, because I begin to realize, you know, that it's hard work, and besides it challenges you — it's enormous. It fascinates you — and if you can just make a quarter of an inch of progress, it's worth all the hours and hours you put into it. The professor told me — he said the problem was a big task, and he gave me something that was bigger than I could do, you know, but he wanted to show me how fascinating research was. He dumped the whole thing in my lap — I mean, he didn't give me a clue where to start, and I just kept asking questions to myself.
> The first thing I did was to comb the abstracts and I found out there that there was very little work done on this problem. In fact,

the only significant work done was in the preparation, and that's all. Now I am trying to understand the mechanism and I realize because I carry out a particular reaction, I can't turn to my professor. I must go home and think it out for myself, and I have to come up with some type of reasoning: "If this is true this particular experiment should happen and then this particular experiment." You try and try over again. It is so enjoyable.

It was the independence, the need to call on his own resources, the discipline and challenge of research that held him. He spoke of the limited time he has:

> Life is short when you think of all there is to do, and especially the things you want to do. I have to discipline my mind to do research. I am doing it now and I realize how difficult it is. It is easy in an experiment. The teacher can judge and correct your work and has a mark down in his little black book, but in research you are on your own. There is nobody for you to ask, what do I do now? If you see something you have to have the ability to interpret it and tie it in with other facts you already know, or devise a new theory. The academic challenge of the sciences is a big challenge, but research is by far a bigger challenge.

"I Had to Forget about These Other Subjects"

In talking about his education, Alex always brought the conversation back to science, and all he had to do. The intensity of his feeling that he "must get on with it," not to finish what he had to do, not to "get somewhere," but to have the chance to work at the unsolved problems, to get near the men who were working at them, to learn how they pursued their quest. He was worried, when applications to graduate schools had gone in, about where he would be admitted:

> It doesn't really matter where I get my degree from — the proof will be, if I can do the work; it won't matter where I come from, you see what I mean? But it's an important thing to have the chance to study under someone who is really first rate. If I could even just once listen to a lecture by Linus Pauling — I just want to hear how he talks about a problem.

Alex was, presumably, getting a liberal education. He was able to immerse himself in the questions posed by science as soon as he discovered that the questions were there to work on and was given a start on ways of working on them. All this was provided that first year at The New College; and his talent for working was fed by the men he studied with from then on.

But for him this was the only important intellectual task he had to do. Like all the New College students he experienced an imaginative freshman program that explored basic questions in other fields as well as science — economic history, literature, philosophy. Many students in that program began to understand the nature of inquiry in these fields that first year. Students made many comments about their work, like the one made by a boy who had never heard of philosophy:

> Well the thing that surprised me, that I discovered, was that a lot of things I had been thinking about weren't only my invention — that a lot of people had been thinking about them too, and that they actually made a part of philosophy. For instance, Plato's philosophy of forms. I had wondered about the same thing myself. What is, and what isn't. Whether anything exists if you don't think about its existence.

The only thing besides the work in physical science that seems to have mattered to Alex was what he learned about writing; and what captured him there was the problem of learning to say *exactly* what you mean. He needed this skill for his study of science — and so it was a skill he wanted to acquire.

For the rest of his studies, then, and so far as one can discover, for the remainder of his college life, working in any other field was a matter of meeting requirements, doing what he had to do in order to be allowed to do what seemed important to him. He grudgingly gave to the study of history, literature, language, what he had to give and no more. He earned top grades in science and mathematics, after the first difficult weeks, and his other grades were mediocre and what he learned insignificant. His anxiety about getting into graduate school came from the fact that, although he had an A average in science, his over-all average was C or B–. "And Caltech accepts so few people — that's the thing."

He studied Latin in his senior year, reading Ovid. He had done rather better in Latin than in other studies in high school. Talking of it he was able only to talk about that part of it that would matter in science:

> I enjoy translating. . . . It is difficult to master the language and be able to say what you want to say in a short space. I find most of the accomplished scientists have this gift. Maybe in disciplining themselves in their field they discipline themselves in being concise and getting across directly. But when I went to my Latin class I saw the difficulty. The teacher is a Harvard scholar, and I suppose very good. But I could say what is being said in less time. Perhaps it is done this way for effect, but it makes me uncomfortable,

and I lose interest. All the time spent in drawing analogies between Ovid and other poets.

None of this meant much to him — neither Latin nor any poetry or other literature he read.

He said he had read some Shakespeare — "a long time ago; I don't remember anything about it." For the rest he read only the literature that was required in the courses he took. He mentioned the *Canterbury Tales, Macbeth, Julius Caesar,* and he found no good reason for studying literature at this time of life when there was so much that needed doing:

> None of it interested me. What are you doing in such studies? The work is there. It's written down. You don't contribute anything. It seems to me this should be done in your leisure. I don't have any leisure. In three years I have taken the required courses. I feel I am taking time out when I do such reading. Maybe when I am 50 or 60, then I will turn to this sort of thing. It is good for a jam session, but you can't have too many jam sessions.

Reading a poem or a play was important when attention was paid to precisely what it said:

> That had a direct effect on my success in the sciences — whether Mr. Acres knows this or not. Because I didn't know how to read, oh no, and because, besides having to have some type of intelligence you have to know how to read the sciences — there are no two ways about it. But other English teachers didn't do this. No, it was just that you had six books to cover and you had to hand in six papers — one every three weeks and we'll cover the course, you see. I liked writing some of the papers, and I did rather well on them. But I never studied much and although I would get good grades on the papers when the final came I would fail the exam and then I would get a C in the course.
>
> But I know I need to be able to appreciate the great works of literature — I know the greatest scientists do. There is Peter Debye now — professor emeritus at Cornell, a Nobel prize winner. "What is your language and I will speak with you," he says. What are the terms you are going to use. Here is a man who walks into all fields . . . I feel he started by trying to understand the sciences, and afterward realized his deficiencies because he was not able to appreciate great literature. I am not able to appreciate it now. If I take time away from my science I will not be able to do as good a job as I want to do. It has to wait, and I know my grades have suffered because of it. Some place the time has to be sacrificed.

But his major objection to the study of both literature and history was that there was no way of finding the truth in these areas of thought:

You read a poem and come into class to discuss it. Sure everybody can say what he thinks, and the teacher can say what he thinks, and sometimes you are expected to accept the idea that what he thinks is the truth. How can you know? Of course people like to sit around and talk about their ideas, but where does it get? In the end you don't know any more about what the writer really meant than you did at the beginning. It seems a waste of time to me.

He was even more skeptical about the study of history. He disliked the way his history course was conducted:

A man comes in and gives a lecture — we don't know how accurate his account is. Why not have a discussion about that? You have to have a curriculum so students will have a general knowledge of what went on. Students should be mature enough to learn about this on their own. Then instead of having a formal lecture you could come into class and discuss your ideas. What would have happened if something had changed? Was this event significant? Was this law good? We had a large lecture group — no questions allowed. I used to do my math homework. It was very discouraging.

He went on to explain that he thought we needed to use all the means at hand for understanding the world we live in:

People in general — we haven't mastered atoms and molecules to explain social behavior. Where else can you start? Study social behavior. What makes people change? History or the social sciences is a good place to start.

But then, when you actually study history it does not seem to move in the direction of resolving such questions:

I ask myself — do you expect to accomplish anything significant? I come up with the answer that all opinions are subjective. You can go through a formal course and give back on an exam 150 dates, you write your thesis and somebody says, "Why was World War I started?" You cannot give any particular reason.

There is some hope for the field of psychology — neither literature nor history can be subjected to the kind of rigorous analysis that is the only way to approach truth, but psychology might be the means through which science will explain social behavior. He remarked that the psychologists have:

these big terms for all types of mental disorders and unbalances in a person, but many of them don't realize how dependent their subject is on physics. When I go into the cafeteria and tell a psychologist that, he says, "You are absolutely out of your mind." I try to explain. Can you be sure that mental disease is *not* caused by some particular chemical substance in the body that is foreign? some substance in a larger dose than it should have, to function normally? This is just a chemical reason, he says — it doesn't explain why somebody wants to kill his mother. I say, How do you know this doesn't explain it?

He is skeptical, too, about mental institutions — whether they really help people. They give sedatives, he says, try counseling, let the patient out when he is not totally cured, and the patient continues to undergo terrific conflicts to confine his feelings and fit the normal pattern of society:

> Let's take this person and see what is different about his system. What compound is present there in larger doses than it should be, and what it takes for this compound to form. How could it form, perhaps a particular gland was oversecreting, perhaps the brain caused the occurrence of this compound which would explain the person. I think social science is directly dependent on physics. Here would be a good place to start.

Politics, like poetry, did not deal with the most important questions, and certainly did not subject itself to rigorous inquiry. He had seen in his neighborhood something of the operation of local political maneuvering:

> I've seen only the sordid side of politics and therefore it has a bad connotation for me. I would rather keep out of it. Maybe if I knew more about it — but from what I've seen I have no interest in it. I realize we have to have some type of organization or group to run this country, but whether the present system is adequate or not I'm not in a position to say.

He was talking about politics and government at the time of the 1962 crisis in United States–Cuban relations:

> I get interested but then I ask myself this question — How much do you know to offer an intelligent answer to this? You can get emotional about it and say we should have invaded Cuba, but have I looked at the whole story? I know I haven't, and realize it is a tremendous responsibility. We are talking about thousands of lives. I am not in a position to say. Of course I get emotionally involved. But you must keep these opinions to yourself.

Alex worked to earn his college expenses all the time he was taking a heavy academic program. He wanted to finish short of four years and went to summer school each summer, working and studying. He came to the study of science in college with nothing to go on — his high school preparation, compared with the kind of work in science many students were getting in good high schools, was almost useless; he had a long way to go, and felt driven by the need to catch up, as he put it.

In spite of this and in spite of his inability to find any interest in ideas outside his immediate concerns, and the failure of other aspects of his education to mean anything to him, he found time to read. He went to the library, he said, whenever he had a chance, and found things to read:

> I like to do this. . . . I look for the big names in science. To see how these men express themselves and how they attack problems. Is what I am doing right — do I have some reason? I am trying to learn how to think in my field. It is not hard to take something specific and learn it, but to understand the type of thinking that was involved.

He listed the places he would like to go for the graduate work he wanted to do — the University of California, Princeton, Chicago, but above all, Caltech. He feared that, in view of his late beginning, his mediocre record outside science, he might not be acceptable to any of them:

> As far as Caltech goes, there isn't much chance. Caltech is probably the best school for this type of thing in the United States.
>
> I tried to meet some of the men at the national meeting in Atlantic City, but they are a special breed. They go by themselves. They are very nice — in fact I sat in on all the talks I could by men from Caltech. They were unbelievable. They had a complete knowledge of their subject. In fact I never forgot one man in particular, Dr. Robinson. He was giving a talk on electron spin resonance. Highly technical, and before he started his talk he gave a half hour elementary on what electron spin resonance was, and this was unbelievable. There were accomplished men there in physics and chemistry and they all listened. The only men at this meeting who could compare with these men from Caltech were the men from Oxford. These are the men who have mastered the theory and all their interest lies in the theory. It opens up the way for the rest of the field. They were young men.

So here is a one-track mind — a wide and deep track, but with no range beyond its single path. A track that had showed no sign of existing a few years earlier. What about this education? He "has no time" for other knowledge or ideas, for experiencing art or problems of human life that cannot be dealt with by science as he understands it. The obvious comment is that nowhere in his academic life, while he was formally meeting the requirements for a liberal education, was anything done to combat this narrowness, to open up more of the world of knowledge and ideas. And it is indeed possible that, had somebody, after that first year, particularly sought to deal with it, he might have had another kind of development. But for one thing, everyone who knew him — and that first year a number of teachers did know him well — knew an immense task was being accomplished in breaking the shell of inertia, distrust of learning, and ignorance about studying and thinking. This they accomplished with him in teaching science; and in teaching him to say on paper "exactly what you mean."

As a liberal education, this education was certainly not a success. It leaves one who reviews it with two questions. How might humanistic studies have fed the development of this boy's mind — as literature fed the development of Scott Hansen's mind (whose interest was, in many ways, not "literary")? And, was Alex perhaps right? Was there perhaps, for him, for his needs, for his intellectual life, indeed no time, in this short span of years, for education in such terms?

The students whose stories are recounted here, and anyone else interested, will know much more in ten years than can be known now of the appropriateness of the education of any one of them. What happened with Alex underlines many of the questions we all have about education in science and the humanities. What happens to him in the future may possibly cast a small light on the problem.

Postscript, March, 1964

PROFESSOR ANDERSON reported of Alex that he was "going great guns" in graduate school — that he had been put right to doing research and was doing well. The letter that came in March to his college says:

> Graduate school is to say the least, very exciting. This is an excellent place for graduate study. Formal course work is kept to a minimum and independent study is strongly encouraged. . . . Most of the students here are from "big name" schools and have cum laude academic records. I feel very lucky to be here. In spite of the keen competition I seem to be holding my own . . . I had to give two seminars to the department. You can imagine how nervous I was lecturing to [he names the distinguished scientists there]; however I was lucky and things went very nicely. The faculty is world renowned. The atmosphere is stimulating and inspiring.
>
> I like experimental work but my heart lies in theory. I have been studying mathematics on my own and I am making good progress. If I can get enough confidence I will probably do a theoretical thesis.

VI

In and Out of Science

THERE is little evidence that the study of science had been important to the intellectual life of the students I talked with. Concerned indeed about man's fate in a world of exploding scientific knowledge, these students, now completing their college life as this book is being written, gave little indication that they had learned much about that world.

Evidence that good students were won to the study of science in college, to become scientists, was even more slight. These students were history and philosophy majors; literature, psychology, and anthropology majors; pre-medical students, and students planning to go into research in science. None of them had decided to be science students after they came to college; a good many had abandoned in college an intention to study science they had come with. And as students with interests in other fields, many of them had strong convictions that the study of science should have been important for them, and they were, at the same time, more critical of the teaching of science than of any other discipline in the curriculum.

Glenn Seaborg stood before two thousand college teachers and administrators that year, talked about what he called the "third revolution" — the present scientific revolution, and of what that revolution means to the education of young people. As chairman of the Atomic Energy Commission he was there as a spokesman for the power the new science wields over men. He talked of the tremendous strides at the borders of the biological and physical sciences (the very field, as it happens, in which the young student Alex Rovere wants to work) and of the fact that biologists will not only soon understand how genetic factors come to exist, but will also learn how to control them. "Man by himself is a relatively puny creature, but his developing technology has steadily served to extend and amplify his range of perception and power."

How far man's knowledge will go is for the scientists to discover; what their discoveries mean to humanity is for all men to know; and if they are to know, they cannot remain in darkness about the discoveries themselves.

This was Dr. Seaborg's message to the men and women educating this generation of college students.

In 1956 Jacob Bronowski wrote:

> Science must become, as a subject, part of our culture, or we shall fail to preserve that culture. The educated man of 1984 will talk the language of science or he will sink to the status of the native yokels when the Normans overran England. By allowing science to be the vocation of the specialists, we are betraying democracy so that it must shrink to what it became in the decline of Athens, when a minority of educated men governed 300,000 slaves. The only way to head off that disaster is to make the educated man universal in 1984.

A large proportion of the students graduating from college in 1962 or 1963 have learned little or nothing of the language of modern science, although Seaborg and Bronowski only underline what has been for ten years, now, a common preoccupation.

Conversations with students and records of what students say give us clues to their thoughts about the two important issues Dr. Seaborg addressed himself to — the education of the future scientists, and the education of men and women who will live in the world the scientists will design. The first group have occupied most of our attention in the past few years; I learned something about prospective scientists, and something about the second group as well, as I talked with students.

The Dedicated Ones

AMONG them were some deeply committed science students like Alex Rovere, and although he was one of the most single-minded, his interest in science was very much like that of the other dedicated ones — they had a passionate attachment to their work, often to the exclusion of other studies, as he excluded other studies. Unlike Alex, most of these students came to college already involved in science, often impatient, and remaining impatient, with other studies. Responding to questions addressed to a group of honors students in a state university about their interest in literature or history, the arts or social sciences, the science students among them repeated Alex's response to the same question — they had no more time for such studies than they were required to spend.

Teachers in liberal arts colleges are often anxious about the encapsulation of science students in the study of science. It is obviously a major responsibility to give scientists the education they will need in a world in which their discoveries will create more and more instruments of power.

Even Robert Oppenheimer, who "raided the place intellectually" as a student at Harvard, said of himself at that time, "I was deeply interested in my science, but I had no understanding of the relations of man to his society." How to educate young scientists to an understanding of what their discoveries will mean to man, and to his relation to his society, is a serious educational task for this generation.

But the question of inducing more students to become scientists has occupied much more of our attention than how to provide a liberal education for those who will. As we "produce" more scientists the problem will grow greater.

What Becomes of the Science Students?

THIS is the second problem. Since the Russian satellite streaked its way beyond the atmosphere, a tremendous literature of research, speculation, and exhortation has come to birth, about the study of science, and the making of scientists. Inquiries into the background and qualities of eminent scientists have already become classics. Writers in popular-science magazines, home magazines, in scientific and educational journals; college presidents, scientists, military officers and science teachers; all are working to win good students to the study of science. Great changes have been made in the teaching of science in the high schools — perhaps greater than many colleges are yet aware of; and hundreds of students seem indeed to be won to science before they enter college.

The students I talked with had been high school students when this intense propaganda got under way in the middle fifties — students who were to be college graduates of 1962 and 1963. More than that, many of them had come to college seriously expecting to be science majors, for the study of science had, in many of their schools, taken on a high glamor. But by the time they reached the second half of their college life the glamor had faded for most of them and no substantial interest in science had taken its place. Alex Rovere made an immense discovery of science in college. Many students, coming to college apparently already committed, were lost to the study of science at the same time.

Of twenty-five superior women students I talked with in a public university, ten had come out of high school expecting to major in science. Half remained, half left science. None of the twenty-five had turned to science from another field. Two had come expecting to go to medical school, and both ended by majoring in philosophy. A third majored in the classics, one in history, one in French — all headed for teaching careers.

It is not only women, and it is not only public universities that have this current history. In a highly competitive urban college 572 students were reported as having changed their majors during college. Of these, 213 left science. Only 24 moved into science from other fields. The records of a class in one of the best of the small private colleges for men show during these same years, that over 21 percent listed science and engineering as their career choice in their applications; which dropped to 17 percent when they became freshmen, and to 4.3 per cent by the time they graduated.

These are the findings of many studies — many students leave the study of science in college, and few enter it from other fields. Most of the students I talked with had entered college in 1958. In May 1959 over two thousand National Merit Scholarship winners and near winners were the subject of an inquiry about changes in their study plans in college. This study, too, reports that among these superior students "the proportion of boys and girls majoring in the natural and biological sciences decreased, while the proportions majoring in the social sciences and humanities increased" — the consequence of students' departure from science for other fields, and of "the failure of the natural sciences to recruit new students."*

Studies completed and under way — and this question will surely be a subject for continuing inquiry — try to discover the fundamental causes in personality, education, or social and economic life which turn students from the study of science. Science professors, "hard" educators and critics of the stamina of the young generally, often say of students that they abandon science because they find the going too hard — they are not able, or not willing, to take the discipline. Surely this must be true of many students — motivation is fragile in many when they come to college, and college often fails to give it sturdier life. But it is less likely to be true of the subjects of this study than of many students. I do not think it was a principal factor in the changes among the students I

---

* Donald D. Thistlethwaite, "College Press and Changes in Study Plans of Talented Students," *Journal of Educational Psychology,* Vol. 51, No. 4, 1960, pp. 222–34.

talked with. Nor did these students have the gloomy image of the scientist revealed by some of the large studies of student opinion — that the scientist is shy, lonely, anti-social, anti-religious, an "egghead" and a generally unattractive fellow; nor of science that it has to be monotonous or boring — although they often feel that much is done to make it so. Nor were they worried, as the studies show some students to be, that they would not make enough money in a scientific career. Nor did any of them say, as students have sometimes said, "For me, training for a career in science is not worth the time and effort required."

Two reasons recurred most often in these conversations for giving up studying science in college, or not choosing to study science. One was that the early years of college opened up new fields of learning, introduced students to new ideas, and made possible other explorations that appear to be more important than the pursuit of mathematics or science even for students who had shown talent in high school for a scientific career, and who had expected to follow one. Scott Hansen was a case in point: with a College Entrance Examination score of 800 in mathematics, he assumed he would be a mathematics student at Harvard, and he was directed to an advanced-placement course. But other interests quickly replaced this assumption, and he asked to be transferred out of an advanced course, so that he could give more time to other studies. "I was able to do it, but I just didn't want to spend that much time with it just then."

"I just found that science wasn't enough," another good student put it. The questions that early in college came to be important to him — and to others — were not dealt with in the study of mathematics or physics. Or perhaps we should say that for some reason the excitement and the importance of science was not communicated to students in the teaching.

But most often the students spoke of the great dissatisfaction with the teaching they had in college. Some had had experiences exactly the opposite of Alex Rovere's — promising and captivating teaching in high school, routine and unimaginative teaching in college. From students in all fields there was more sharp criticism of the teaching of science in college than the teaching in any area of the curriculum except the courses in education. They spoke of interest kindled in high school, soon destroyed in college. Two Merit Scholarship students in a liberal arts college found the study of science dull and pedestrian, compared to their expectations, and even their experience. One left the college he had chosen for another where he hoped to find science more vital; and the other shifted his major.

The *intention* to study science continues strong. A study of Merit Scholars of 1958 indicated that more than three-quarters of the boys who were finalists or scholars that year said they wanted to go into pure or applied science.* It would be valuable to know how many of those who graduated in June 1962 still planned on scientific careers.

Anxious observers, viewing the failure of science to attract enough good students, are most alarmed by the loss of "science manpower" in a world that needs scientists. This is serious to be sure. There is an equally important reason for dismay at the failure of other students — students of literature and history, philosophy and the arts — to have, in these creative and flexible years of their lives, any experience with this new knowledge. The failure is not only in the scientists lost to science, but in the intelligent and imaginative men and women for whom all this knowledge of this new world is lost.

Often even students who said they knew they had learned something from a course in science or mathematics learned with no enlargement of vision; imagination was not touched, nor the significance and the possibilities of modern science realized. A good student, now studying law, said:

> I've studied mathematics as a science. I took two science courses because they were required, but I enjoyed them, and they fulfilled an interest in science I'd had since high school. I would say that that was important to my education — it trained me in methodical thinking and attention to details. It can be a very challenging course of study — but I found it lacking the life or excitement that I found in the social sciences.

The first important fact of Alex Rovere's experience with science in college was that a chemistry teacher taught him how to stop memorizing and begin to think. Too many bright students missed such teaching:

> Perhaps I wanted too much out of the course; I wanted the problems and arguments in the field at the same time I mastered the basic material. I generally felt that the time spent memorizing various information for weekly quizzes and other blackboard games was wasted. . . . I took a one-semester course in physics for non-majors. This course I looked forward to with great enthusi-

* Paul F. Brandwein and others, "Creativity and Personality in the Scientist," *National Society for the Study of Education Yearbook*, 1960, Part I, pp. 63–81.

asm, as I had been reading works about and in physics and enjoyed them, very much. I also had a very strong feeling that if I were to go into politics or any related field, I would need to know as much as possible about science — and especially about physics. In order to avoid a course of formula-memorizing of the regular physics course, this one was taught without most of that and with very little to replace it, except descriptive lectures about the various tools and instruments used in physics. The same is true of chemistry — there is a course for majors and a course for the more ignorant. But science has to be such an important part of our life today that it cannot afford to be treated this way.

A number of these students looked for opportunities to work in science. John Furness, who had almost no motivation for any of the work he had to do in high school, wanted to find out what went on in a research laboratory, so he applied for a student's place in a cancer-research institute. This was in the summer between school and college. "We had nine or ten weeks of lectures in the biological sciences — lots of students got interested there in studying science. It was exciting and the prospect of studying science was exciting." But for him this interest quickly disappeared in college.

Those who left science found that, as they experienced it, "science wasn't enough"; that the questions they found important in college were not dealt with in the study of mathematics or physics. These often were students who had talent and skill which made it possible for them to perform well in classrooms and laboratories:

> I studied physics for a year. I got the notion in high school that this was a subject I could dig into, and work at important problems. I got A in the course — it was never any trouble. But it was never any good either — neither the professor nor the lab man was interested in the questions I wanted to ask, and I got tired of the routine. It took me another year to find out where I was going, and now I'm majoring in philosophy. But I still think the questions I *can* ask in philosophy could have been asked in physics, too. I just never got the chance.

Edgar Friedenberg has a revealing study of a large number of students who were majoring in science, or had intended to do so, but left. It tells the same story as my smaller number, who were not chosen for their past or present interest in science.

> Those of our best subjects who left did so because of the way scientists are taught and the way they are used; not because of

what science essentially is. After all, it is our respondents who believe that science deals with deep and fundamental issues of being, who are correct. But undergraduates do not get much chance to get down to fundamentals.*

These pages are not written to join the anxious appeals of the men who tell us we need more scientists to run the new physical universe, or to win races to the moon, or wield the power of arms.

When the telescope was invented, the skies explored, the globe circumnavigated, the poets and the scholars who contemplated the new world were filled with hope and fear:

> All things that move between the quiet poles
> Shall be at my command...

Marlowe, who consorted with the men who were making the new world visible, had a tremendous sense of the power and possibility of the new knowledge. For John Donne "The New Philosophy calls all in doubt." We are experiencing again cause for the hopes and the doubts.

But there were then no millions of young people with access to the new knowledge; there was no chance of achieving a general understanding of what the new science was, what it might become, and what it might accomplish. For our students the tremendous chance has scarcely begun to be exploited.

* Edgar Friedenberg, "Why Students Leave Science," *Commentary,* August, 1961, p. 155.

VII

Anna Warren at Sarah Lawrence

THE daughter of parents born in Europe, who had great interest in the outdoors and in physical activity, Anna Warren lived outside a small, comfortable New England town, in a home surrounded by fourteen acres of wooded country. She lived in the same house all her life, until she came to college, and she went to the local elementary and high schools.

She needed a scholarship; she applied to three private colleges for women, all in the East, and was accepted by all of them. When she decided to come to Sarah Lawrence College her high school principal wrote (to the college, not to the parents), "You lucky people."

"You Lucky People"

To the extent that the college was looking for intelligent, highly motivated students, who were also questioning, sensitive to the complexities of learning, it was not altogether lucky. By her own account she was "dying" to come to college and learn. It was easy for her to achieve a kind of quick, superficial excellence, and she did. She was finally able to go beyond obvious acquisitive accomplishment and she did, but learning how to achieve this came slowly.

Her education is a good illustration of how some intelligent students need to learn how to go beyond good formal learning to achieve a personal intellectual relation with ideas and knowledge; and the difficulties they sometimes have in the process. It illustrates, too, how ideas a student encounters early and recognizes in some dim way as important, return and develop, as knowledge and understanding grow. She came early to some vague notions about human and social values, and one can follow the way these ideas, as she learned how to learn, became sharper.

Anna's College Entrance Examination scores were good, but not remarkable — the linguistics score was 649, the mathematics score 508. About school she wrote in her application to college:

The general feeling I have towards my twelve years of public schooling is that I have hardly ever felt truly challenged. Everything in school seemed to be almost too easy. In almost everything I have done I feel there was always more I could do and learn. Therefore I looked for more intellectual stimulation outside of school — art, books, and interesting people. I enjoyed school quite a bit, and have gotten on very well with the great majority of my teachers and fellow students.

The admissions director of the college commented on her "easy, informal manner, as if all the adults she knew had treated her well and she was expecting to be liked."

As a child she studied art and music, but her main interest outside of school was dance. None of the arts was important as part of her school work, but she studied ballet for five years. She performed in plays at school, and in high school she thought she would like to "take part in some branch of theatre after college, either dance or drama, or a combination." She came to Sarah Lawrence expecting to study dance, but at the same time she said she wanted a college degree and a Master's degree "so I will be able to teach some day." The unusual opportunity at Sarah Lawrence College to study dance and other performing arts as part of an academic program made the choice of this college seem especially appropriate.

"She Never Lets Up for a Moment"

HER response to a question on the admissions form asking her to name the person she most admires is revealing because as a student she lacked the very quality she said she most admired; and this lack stood longest in the way of her education. She said of Melissa Hayden, ballerina of the New York City Ballet:

> When I have seen her dance, she has given "all"; she never lets up for a moment on stage. When I have seen her I have felt a personal communication that remains in my mind long after the memory of the maybe more technical brilliance of someone like Maria Tallchief.

This wish to care about what one is engaged in, the admiration for people who immerse themselves in what they do and think, appeared often in her conversation, her account of her own education, and the papers she wrote about writers, philosophers, political figures, or scientists. And at the same time her own tendency to remain outside what she was learning, not probe, not become immersed, was the most serious hindrance to her own education, and the most difficult to overcome. Teachers tried to deal with this in a variety of ways, but it took a long time for her to overcome it.

Like every interesting education, this one developed an individual design as it progressed. Her education moved along two lines, related, but not perceived by her as related — perhaps not perceived by her at all. One had to do with the way she responded to her studies; the other with attitudes and ideas that kept recurring in her discussions and her writing about what she studied.

The first was her slow growth away from routine, acquisitive learning, toward serious engagement in her intellectual life. The other was her effort to discover unity, or wholeness, in people and situations; and the manifestations of growth and wholeness in the social structure, in science, or in poetry.

I found in most students whose education was more than an accumulation of credits — who felt and communicated the sense of four years of intellectual growth — the emergence of an internal shape or consistency to their learning. The obvious explanation of this is the existence of a major — one comes to concentrate one's interest on American history, or literature, or mathematics.

The design I am talking about involves something more than a major. It emerges in the way a student uses what he is learning, in whatever field. It is a kind of intellectual configuration, a ruling passion, or a way of looking at, of thinking and feeling about, all sorts of ideas and subjects. The presence of this pervasive *internal* design in a student's education accounts partly at least for the great difference that exists in the education of two students who study the same subjects — have the same majors, comparable intellectual ability.

Such a design is created, little by little, when studies have vitality for students, cause them to inquire or speculate, so that they come to ask, of anything they study, certain kinds of questions that begin to characterize their cast of thought. They repeatedly look for light on these questions, sometimes consciously, sometimes not; but reading papers they write over a period of years, listening to them talk about the life of their studies, reveals these central preoccupations many times.

Great teachers with a compelling point of view about life or events sometimes affect this direction a student's education takes, whatever he may study; often, I think, it is the student's own inner needs or drives, either for self-understanding or for accomplishment, that bend what he studies in a direction that affects his growth, whether he quite knows it or not; sometimes it is a student's private convictions, about religion or society or politics.

But whatever the cause, it is worth observing that when one tries to trace minutely the experience of a student all the way through college, one is apt to find a kind of core or propelling central force to his thinking which determines how he uses what he is learning, and, more specifically, what he chooses to explore.

One can probably discover this internal design more readily in the education of students in institutions that allow them some choice about what they will study, and some choice about what they will do *within* the framework of a course. It is probably revealed more vividly when students have a chance to write substantial papers and to have a voice in what they will write about, than in places where what students have accomplished in a course is uncovered by examinations only.

By the usual academic standards Anna Warren was a superior student. Her high school record was high, she was described by teachers as a consistent worker who was always thoroughly prepared. "She ranks high in the eyes of all her teachers because she can be counted on to get her work done." In one way this record continued in college. She is repeatedly described as reading widely, working conscientiously at all tasks required of her. The official record of her reading and of the papers she wrote in the four years is impressive.

Teachers report on students in greater detail at Sarah Lawrence than in most colleges, and a full official record exists of the judgments of Anna's teachers and her adviser about her work as a student. These records include written reports sent to the students; confidential comments written for the use of advisers and the administration; reports by advisers; minutes of any meetings of the Committee on Student Work in which a student might have been discussed; and academic ratings of both capacity and achievement, used for graduate school or transfer purposes. These rating scales are the nearest approach to grades used by the college. As a freshman Anna was rated by one teacher as good-to-excellent in performance and good-to-outstanding in ability; by a second as excellent in performance and outstanding in ability. The ratings on the third course were lower — an exception I will say something about later. Her adviser (with whom she was also taking a history course) describes her as "my best freshman student. She has initiative, sustained interest, curiosity, capacity to read difficult books and voracious appetite for more."

The Road from One Kind of Excellence to Another

ANNA'S reports remain good throughout the next two years, and in her senior year she is rated as having done excellent work, and is judged as outstanding in ability (top ratings in both cases) by one teacher; good-to-excellent in performance and good-to-outstanding in ability by a second; as good in performance and good-to-outstanding in ability by a third. These ratings of the senior year *look* the same as the ratings of the freshman year. So all "A"s look alike, although they stand for a vast variety of qualities and accomplishments.

It is the descriptive reports, written several times each year, that reveal the development of the students and the kind of work they do, reveal, as in the case of Anna, that the ratings of the freshman year mean something qualitatively quite different from the same ratings in the senior year. What these teachers have to say in these descriptive reports reflects the difference.

In the midst of the consistently high praise of this student by the teachers in her high school is one skeptical comment:

> The only reservations I have about her are difficult to express. Behind her fine qualities I don't feel a great depth or capacity for a really passionate involvement in life. There is a brittleness, a certain self-conscious chill in her approach. This, however, may say more about me than about her.

It does say a good deal about the teacher, whose aims for education are obviously penetrating, as well as high in the conventional way; and it says a good deal about Anna, too — a student about whose general intelligence no one raises a question, who works steadily and hard, who wants to be educated, and who came to college wanting to study dance, and wanting to become a teacher. We remember that she admired the ballet dancer Melissa Hayden because she gives "all" when she dances, and creates, for her, the observer, "a personal communication."

The principal problem in her own education, recognized by the high school teacher, and commented on one way or another by teachers many times in college, was to achieve exactly what she admired in Miss Hayden — the capacity to experience fully what she learned, and to make it part of herself. She needed to learn not to remain outside what she learned, not to be satisfied with learning *about* what she was studying, but to probe and question. Although her work was always good by

most standards, it was not until her senior year that she came to understand how the accomplishments of other people — writers and scientists — grew out of their total involvement, the kind of attachment to
their work the perceptive high school teacher missed in her; and to experience something of that attachment herself. She found it also in certain teachers who by their example taught her the difference between
formal and fully experienced learning.

At the same time, the ideas of poets and philosophers that interested her most in her studies had to do with *their* effort to find unity,
artistic structure, in the universe, or to express their feelings about it, or
to communicate the idea to others. The words "organic," "organic
growth," "unity," recur in the papers she writes; and she chooses to
write about individuals and movements devoted to such concepts. She
copes with these ideas whether she is writing about Wordsworth, Transcendentalism, Captain Ahab, the idea of democracy in education, or
the history of Charles Darwin's creative life. This is the internal design
this student's education developed as she went through the four years.

In a letter she wrote the year after she had taken a senior seminar
called "Studies in Theory Building" she described her own sense of this
discovery, slowly approached, and finally made. She had spent most of
the semester studying the development of Charles Darwin's theory of
evolution:

> What I remember most about the seminar was the *process* of
> writing the paper on Darwin . . . it was then that all the rather am-
> biguous discussions we had had on the creative process began to
> make sense — it was going through the creative process myself as
> I discovered Darwin's process — it was being on the inside, of see-
> ing from within. Before that I had been seeing Darwin from the
> outside even as I was reading his works and taking notes — though
> I remember I didn't take many notes — it was while I was writing
> that I had to re-read everything, and as I was building a structure
> for my paper and as it developed, it was then that I realized Dar-
> win's incredible development. The amount of work he did and the
> amazing detail was what was most impressive — the years and
> years of observing, experimenting, cataloguing, always accumu-
> lating more and more information — and as he accumulated so
> much, the power of the idea of evolution grew and grew in him un-
> til it had to be propounded . . . it had to come forth.
>
> The whole meaning of creativity was changed for me too — I
> had always known that creativity implied growth — that some-
> thing new that hadn't been before had been created, had in a sense,

"grown." But as the direct outcome of what had been before —
this I hadn't thought of very much as a part of creative experience — of emerging from and relating to what is — and something new happening, though this was latent in me and I did believe in it in a vague kind of way. However, I still was seeing and
feeling creativity as an intuitive, apocalyptic experience — of
something "happening" — of the shining light suddenly bursting
forth. I'd even written papers on this — on Keats's theories of
poetry, on revelation in the Old Testament, . . . this is what at-
tracted me to Romantic literature, the creation of art through inspiration, through a super-intuition.

But it was with the Darwin paper that I began to realize the
amount of work that goes into creativity, that it involves both
dedication to the task at hand, and also a relationship between inspiration and empirical fact, rational thought, and plain hard
work. Of course I had always "known" that being a great artist
involved an incredible amount of hard work, and the years it often
took to write a book, but usually we see only the finished product
— the ballet performance, or the poem on the page. But it was going through Darwin's letters and notebooks that gave me a real
sense of the true process behind a great creative act. It was seeing
from within — in the true sense of the word — because even when
we analyze a poem and we do enter into the poem, it is still the
poem as a poem, not the poet as creator one knows, and it is in this
larger sense that the work on Darwin was so valuable.

This is where her education finally took her.

The first year she studied European history, literature, and dance,
and along with the work in dance the auxiliary studies of the performing
arts — costume design and execution, music for dance, stage design.
Anna had been active in theatre and dance performance in her high
school years, all of it outside her regular program:

> I worked and I got A's in high school, but everything I did dur-
> ing high school that I was interested in was outside of school. I was
> interested in theatre and plays. I was in summer stock. This was
> exciting. I was on stage.

The record of the first year at college describes this bright student's
relation to learning, her assets and liabilities. A history paper on a Ren-
aissance figure, Marsilio Ficino, illustrates the character of her work.
She read a great deal for it, she collected a large amount of information
about the intellectual life of the time, read what the historians had to say
about the man. The paper was a thorough if not a thoughtful digest of

all she had read. It was a good freshman paper by standards not only accepted but generally encouraged in freshmen: her sources were sound, what she learned was well put together, it was well-documented; a catalogue of her subject's ideas. And the paper was warmly praised for these virtues. What it lacked, what the teacher did not ask for, and what she could not have produced, in this instance, was question or speculation.

The literature teacher, too, reporting at the end of the year says he finds, on reviewing his notes about her work, that he has used repeatedly such words as "clean," "lucid," "strong straight-line exposition."

Later, just out of college, looking back on her freshman year, she said "I read a great deal; I was in control of what I was doing; I got everything done on time — but I think the sophomore year was the real beginning."

She was praised for the virtues teachers usually praise students for, and are glad when they find them in freshmen. But the work in dance — the field in which her pleasures principally came, when she was in high school — was a failure. Her performances in the dance workshop were described by the faculty as "very fine; the ability is there; she moves well; has intelligence." But the basic results were mediocre. She was described as quick to grasp ideas and suggestions and "has learned how to make them work for her," but in the end "her work for the year is satisfactory only because she is sufficiently gifted and intelligent to get by." "Her work is superficial, the studies brief and thin. She lived on her wit; from time to time she made a real effort and produced something good, then seems to become satisfied with herself."

The record here reminds one of the remark of the high school teacher — "a brittleness, a self-conscious chill." The work in dance demanded immediate involvement and imagination for success — especially the success of a talented girl — and this demand she could not meet.

Four years later she recalled her feelings about the experience in the dance classes, and there is no doubt that the contrast between the demands of ballet and the demands of modern dance she was now exposed to was great:

> The disappointment of studying dance at Sarah Lawrence was so great precisely because this was the field I expected to get most involved in. . . . I remember the contorted, muscle-straining exercises we had to perform — a far cry from the lyricism, strength and beauty of the ballet I loved so much. . . . I clammed up.

What was required here was something more than the development of skill, and hard work to acquire it. It is part of the history of her education that it was to take time, and the repeated example and stimulus of unusual teachers, to help her meet these larger demands. That year she neither satisfied her teachers nor had any pleasure or sense of accomplishment in her dance studies. After that year she abandoned them and turned her attention to other fields.

"It Is a Philosophy that Refuses the False Comforts of Absolutes"

HER first awareness that there was another way of learning, came in her second year. As part of a plan to acquire a solid background of knowledge, she registered for a course that looked to her rather like a survey of English literature, although one with an uncommon design. Virginia Woolf's *Orlando* was the starting place; and literary works of other periods were read as discussion grew out of this book. The teacher of the course was a poet (there is something to be said for poets rather than literary historians teaching the history of literature); and it was lucky for this particular student that the teacher insisted relentlessly that she discover, if at all possible, what the experience of reading poetry could be:

> The first assignment we had was out of *Orlando* — we were to write about the nature of a particular experience. I went into conference and she tore the thing apart, said I had no sense of what was immediate, specific.
>
> We studied enough Anglo-Saxon so we could see how the language was made, and she had us translate 50 or 60 lines of Beowulf. I got the paper back — there were parts I had missed, and she took this as an indication that I had holes in my character, that I would skip over things. This really frightened me. She made me go back and do it over again. I do know that I have felt that if I don't want to bother with something I do skip over it — it is too much trouble. You can't read poetry that way. She shook people like that all the time.

For the individual studies students undertake in such courses, she spent most of a semester reading John Keats. She made her start, when it came to writing about Keats, from a phrase of his, "negative capability." He had used it in a letter to his brothers: *

* I believe she encountered this phrase in an introduction to the edition she used. It was not so much her discovery of the phrase that is important, as her use of it.

"at once it struck me what quality went to form a Man of Achievement, especially in Literature, and which Shakespeare possessed so enormously — I mean *Negative Capability,* that is, when a man is capable of being in uncertainties, mysteries, doubts, without any irritable reaching after fact and reason."

It was a step ahead that this orderly and unquestioning student should have chosen to write on such a subject. It was her first experience with learning as a quest rather than an acquisition:

The state of Negative Capability that Keats describes is one in which a man has the ability to deal intellectually and emotionally with the meanings of uncertainty, mystery, doubt, i.e. the unknown. The further the poet can extend into the realms of the unknown 'without any irritable reaching after fact and reason,' the more the imagination is stimulated to assume a greater awareness of existence....

Negative Capability allows the mind to consider all, without passing unnecessary moral judgments as to what is good or evil; it does not sentimentally and romantically eliminate and simplify, but is a difficult state of thinking and imagining that considers all factors that affect human existence. . . . It is a philosophy that refuses to recognize the false comforts of absolutes; it lives in the skeptical uncertainties of half-knowledge, contradictions, of the paradoxes of good and evil, love and death, wisdom and sorrow.

She had planned a junior year in France, and so she registered that fall for a course in French literature; but as the year proceeded she discovered she needed to stay where she was — the reasons for studying in France were never very firm, and grew weaker as she began to recognize that her education was getting under way. The shift in the way she was learning, started in the literature class, was carried on in a course in American history. It was a course in intellectual history and social philosophy as well. After the first semester an American literature course replaced the French literature; this gave her an opportunity in both history and literature courses to study ideas that were forming American life and thought in the nineteenth century. She read Emerson and Thoreau in the history course, as well as the important political writers from the Revolution on, and she read Hawthorne, Whitman, and Melville, as well as some twentieth-century American writers.

Of first importance for the development of her education was a study of Transcendentalism which, like the paper on Keats later that year, required her to try to understand the meaning of the ideas and knowledge men have at their disposal, as well as to know what they are.

The writings of Emerson and Thoreau especially had a twofold appeal for her; and her interest in them illustrates her preoccupation with certain ideas that persisted throughout her education: the interest in the idea of unity, or wholeness, in life, and the idea of change. Interest in such ideas as they affect personal and social life is common enough in reflective young people; it was peculiarly important in Anna Warren's intellectual experience. She was a good student, successful in commonly accepted terms, whose education in college was a slow departure from preoccupation with merely acquiring knowledge to a preoccupation with how men develop, and how they seek a center or core or sense of unity in life. Like other students at Sarah Lawrence College, she had a wide range of choice in reading within the structure of her courses; and a review of what writers she chose to write about, and what subjects she chose for her individual studies traces these preoccupations more clearly than we can ordinarily trace them in the history of a student's education.

"A Passionate Commitment Not Only to Teaching but to Life, and They Communicated This to Their Students"

ANNA WARREN'S junior year enlarged her understanding of how her education should proceed, although she was not able to see what was happening until later. She was not again to be satisfied with the kind of learning that had satisfied her when she came. But more important than the subjects she studied that junior year was what had been accomplished for her by the kind of teaching she had had in her second year, and the ideas she dealt with in the papers she wrote. She said a great deal about the teaching of poetry and of history, and about the teachers who taught her that second year:

> They were different in so many ways — but they were alike in having a passionate commitment not only to what they were teaching, but to life — and they communicated this sense to their students. It was already true of me that the best work I did was what I did in conference, in most cases. But in the poetry course I couldn't separate out what I did — the impact of her was in everything I studied, and I still remember it vividly. The Keats paper I spent a whole semester on — I finally began to learn what it was to read poetry; and I knew better, because of that, what I was doing in the Victorian course the next year.

She describes the junior year as an "about face" in the way she studied. The explosive period was over, and she put to good use what she had learned about reading fully, and with care:

> I have a feeling that your whole life is a sort of process of learning how to read, and you have to know how to read different things different ways. That second semester of the second year was my best time, academically. I worked all the time, because there was suddenly so much. Going in to the Victorian poetry course was exactly right for me, after that, because it slowed me down, and I was beginning to be able to use what I had learned. We read little, and read it carefully. Teaching is a more deliberate thing for this man than for the others who had been so important the year before. He knows how to contain a class; each one was a gem as far as structure was concerned. You read line by line, until you came to possess the poem.

A philosophy course was useful to her, but her judgment of it was also a mark of how far she had moved in two years. It had much of the quality of the history course that had been so successful the first year — a systematic study of the principal figures in Western thought:

> It was basic — it gave you a structure to hang things on, and it gave you the structure of the development of Western thought. I can place things in time. The course was thoroughly organized, it was good; it was useful. It had to include too much, and I didn't really learn *that* much. What philosophy, in a way (I'm not talking about it as an academic subject) what philosophy ought to mean to you, it didn't mean to you studying it that way. You were not really involved in the philosophical ideas that were discussed — you were learning to know who said what. For me it would have been better to have it as a freshman or a sophomore — that junior year I was impatient for something different, because I had learned to look for something different.

For Anna the senior year was a genuine culmination, and the work she did was evidence that she had slowly come to understand what a creative experience in education can mean.

The seminar in philosophy called "Studies in Theory Building" was an analysis of the processes leading to the discovery, or creation, of new concepts and theories. The principal figures studied were Freud, Darwin, and Marx. A good deal of information exists about each man in the form of letters, other autobiographical information, and other writings which enable students to re-create the intellectual journey leading to the formation of original ideas. How does the creative thinker function? Anna spent the semester working mainly on Charles Darwin.

Another seminar, "Ideas in America," in which much time was given to the place of the theory of evolution in American thought, led her to spend most of her time on a study of education, and in a third course, she wrote on the hero and the anti-hero in modern literature.

That part of Anna Warren's education which was not a child's routine performance of tasks set by a teacher, but a serious reflection of what she had discovered and what she believed, began in her second year with the paper on Transcendentalism and was intensified by the reading of Keats. It was from Keats that she began to learn about the importance of a man learning "to deal intellectually and emotionally with the meanings of uncertainty, mystery, doubt, i.e. the unknown . . . a philosophy that refuses to recognize the false comforts of absolutes."

Every important paper she wrote from her second year on — which means, in the way a student's work is designed at that college, papers growing out of sustained individual studies, supported by individual discussions with teachers — bore on the question of how a man seeks a shape or unity in life, not by conformity or the acceptance of conventional beliefs, but by inquiry and search. She chose to write on the Transcendentalists, and a large part of this paper dealt with the particular absolutes of Puritanism which the Transcendentalists sought to escape. The concepts of growth, change, development, became central to her thinking whatever she studied, and this preoccupation had the obvious result of shifting her education from the performance of tasks and the accumulation of knowledge to inquiry and exploration.

She read Emerson and Thoreau, and found in *Walden* Thoreau's preoccupation with the "organic principle," which, applied to man "implies the great potential in humanity." She studied ideas about leadership in a democratic society, and read Woodrow Wilson on constitutional government. From Wilson she took this passage as a starting point:

> Democracy is wrongly conceived when treated merely as a body of doctrine, or a form of government. It is a stage of development. . . . Its process is experience, its meaning national organic unity and effectual life. It comes, like manhood, as the fruit of youth: immature peoples cannot have it and the maturity to which it is vouchsafed is the maturity of freedom and self-control and no other.

Reading her papers one finds many times she has selected out of her reading ideas and passages referring to the search to discover "organic unity" in life; although it is unlikely that she was aware of this preoccupation herself, in the process of her education. She chooses to write about Wordsworth — the child's unity with nature, the "perfection of unity with the natural world," the loss and separation that comes with manhood, when "he can *remember* the unity of the inner and the outer life, even though in actual life the split between feeling and thought is ever deepening." He "searches for something to replace the loss of the sense of unity, besides the mere remembrance of it . . . He communicates in the poetry some of the vital changes and conflicts as they were made manifest in his personal life — the passionate union of sense and mind in youth, the growing split between mind and nature, between the inner and outer life"; and she traces the history of his search to rediscover what he had lost.

She wrote about the hero and the anti-hero in nineteenth-century literature, about Ahab's single-mindedness, his fierce defiance, "a *modern* Promethean who cannot defy on the basis of an ordered universe such as the ancient Prometheus could; rather Ahab's rebellion is within a chaotic, unordered, irrational world." The other literary characters she writes about are "divided men," and it is the element of division, of failure to find unity either in the self or in the outer world that turns the classically conceived hero into the anti-hero. In Camus's Dr. Rieux, alone among the central figures in the novels she writes about, she finds a resolution:

> He is heroic in his commitment to his fellow men, to preserving life, to saving men. He knows that the plague is in all men and that it will return. There is never a firm victory over the plague, and it will reappear when least expected. But Rieux has a true faith in man and in the healers of the world, those who "unable to be saints but refusing to bow down to pestilences, strive their utmost to be healers." Rieux's faith in man and his own image of man is affirmed when he says that what we learn in the time of pestilence is that "there are more things to admire in men than to despise." Here the modern hero emerges from the depths of the anti-hero in a unique statement of the significance and worth of man in the world today.

Anna studied also, in her final year, with the teacher of her sophomore year, when she began her studies of American life and thought and read and wrote about the Transcendentalists. The second association was in the seminar called "Ideas in America." The teacher of the course was himself interested in problems of education in a democracy, and as Anna began asking more questions of herself and others that had implications for education, she undertook to read a wide variety of writers on education — Whitehead, Dewey, Matthew Arnold, de Tocqueville; she returned to Emerson; poets and novelists who wrote about education — D. H. Lawrence, Robert Frost, Whitman, T. S. Eliot; and philosophers who wrote of language and meaning — Cassirer and Susanne Langer.

A famous passage from Whitehead (discovered anew by her) is the theme of her thoughts and comments about education:

> The students are alive, and the purpose of education is to stimulate and guide their self-development. It follows as a corollary from this premise, that the teachers also should be alive with living thoughts. This whole book is a protest against dead knowledge, that is to say, against inert ideas.

It was the most important lesson Anna had to learn in college, and she spent much of her time learning it. From her high school days she had always worked "thoroughly" at whatever she undertook to do, taking in, accumulating notes, putting information together in an orderly way. She had been learning in the process of her own education that the important thing about one's relation to other men's ideas does not rest with knowing what they are, but what difference they make to the individual who discovers them:

> The reading process *is* education; and so what we read and how we read it assumes great importance.

Her preoccupation with meaning, and with the impact on the individual of what he reads, drew together the impressions and discoveries about her own education. Two teachers had taught her something about how to read poetry, and she began now in the "Ideas in America" seminar, and in "Studies in Theory Building," to learn something about both the process she had been through and how it had shaped her education. She had begun, also in that second year of her education, to learn what some of the central ideas were that lay at the root of American democracy. When she undertook for this senior seminar to find out something about the processes of education, what she had learned about the reading of poetry, and what she had learned about the nature of democracy, from de Tocqueville and Whitman and Thoreau, came together.

This process also illustrates what takes place in a student's learning when he has had a chance to deal first, and in detail, with the primary material, itself. He understands, by the fullest direct contact with creative thinkers — as far as he is able to with his limited knowledge, — the idea of Transcendentalism, or the character of a hero, or the possible meaning of a line of poetry. And then, when he has become practiced, in however halting a way, in knowledge of a poet's metaphors, or the design of a man's religious faith, or philosophical belief, he can turn to the theoretical critics, or the practitioners, who can provide him with what they know as a context for understanding what he has been through, for seeing what the experience of poetry, of ideas, signifies for his own view of the world.

"Darwin's Letters and Notebooks Gave Me a Sense of the True Process Behind a Great Creative Act"

THIS coming together and intensifying of the accumulated experience of her education in college took on added dimension — and perhaps the most important one — in a seminar in Anna's senior year, the same year she was studying ideas in America, and learning something about the process of education beyond her own experience. The seminar took the students behind the experience most of them had been having in their studies of writers, philosophers, political thinkers — the experience of knowing (and it is to be hoped, understanding) a creative thinker's view of man and the world. What the students were confronted with here was the task of re-creating, by their own understanding, the processes by which men who had made significant contributions to concepts of human nature, or the physical world, or the social order, came by their ideas.

To the extent that the student does re-create them, the experience has a two-fold importance for him. Discovery for himself of the steps that led a man to a new system of thought provides an association with his ideas, a kind of knowledge of them, that an acquaintance with the theory that finally emerged does not give. But in addition, the process of trying to retrace these steps toward discovery — learning, even if dimly, what is involved in creation — gives to him himself, at least in small measure, the creative experience, as he follows the footsteps of the creator.

Anna spent much of her time that semester retracing the path of Darwin's research, and the union between his research and his life:

> To find out how Darwin's attitudes and mental habits were shaped, we must look to his *Autobiography,* which he wrote in 1876 for his children, and also to his *Letters* which give an intimate view of Darwin's thinking throughout his life.

This is where she began. And she started with his own account of the "only qualities that gave any promise for his future brilliance in scientific work" — as he describes himself, "my strong and diversified tastes, much zeal for whatever interested me, and a keen pleasure in understanding any complex subject or thing."

She made a point of Darwin's description of his schooling, "the method of learning by memorization," which he found sterile and without meaning; and points out that his real learning about natural phenomena came from explorations he and his friends made apart from his formal studies.

She followed him on the *Beagle,* his observations and his notes, paid attention to the joy observation brought him, apart from where these observations would lead. "He is the inveterate observer who cannot wait to record what he has just seen," and he speaks of looking forward to writing it down, when he has seen something that gives him pleasure. But she saw, too, "in his direct, unpretentious style of writing . . . the extraordinary thoroughness of the workings of his mind and the methodical, yet unpedantic, way in which he presented his researches and observations."

It is a fortunate student who can follow, at whatever distance, the road a creative man travels toward creation. At each point in his career of discovery she follows the connection between what he had been doing, what emerged, how he communicated the events to himself in his notebooks and to others in correspondence, how the responses related to his own thinking and the next steps he was engaged in. Such retracing of Darwin's steps as can be done from the written record prompts the idea that the particular studies he made, his reflections, and intermediate conclusions grew one out of another; and that the true dimensions of the grand plan of his thought came slowly as what newly emerged fit what he had observed and thought before.

Anna Warren's observations about the way a creative mind moved toward a great discovery gave her only a glimpse of the process; but it was a tremendous asset to her education. It marked the end of descriptive, repetitive learning, and fixed her attention on the process of creation rather than on "the finished poem."

It was a large advance for her as a future teacher. The way of learning she had left behind will not bind her in her teaching; and the kind of learning that meant "being on the inside, seeing from within," will alert her to the importance of creating in her students such an attitude earlier in their intellectual history than it came in hers.

Postscript, March, 1964

ANNA WARREN is taking a master's degree in an experimental internship program preparatory to going into high school teaching, attending seminars and teaching under supervision in a high school. She had had more than a semester of work when she wrote:

> The teachers I'm working with are great — I'm on the "senior team" with the head of the English department and one other experienced teacher, and it is very helpful to be working so closely with two good, experienced teachers.

She thinks the high school students are getting much more than they used to:

> I'll be teaching *Heart of Darkness* this year — how much they will get out of it I don't know, but at least the challenge will be there for those who are able to meet it, which wasn't true when I was in high school. The students here will get earlier something I missed. I had to get so much in college, and I feel lucky that I got so much at a time when I needed so much. I only hope I am able to give some of this to my students — and that somehow in their future they will have opportunities to develop this.

VIII

We Still Need Teachers — Face to Face

FACE to face means many different things. The encounter of teachers and students may take place in a small room, around a table, and it may occur in a large class, in which teacher and students do not talk to or with each other in the classroom. But whatever the size of the class, it means there has been communication between the teachers and the students that satisfies both teachers and students that they have been heard, and their words considered. Joseph Katz, writing about "Personality and Interpersonal Relations in the Classroom," in *The American College,* tells of the teacher who worked hard and long, prepared his lecture notes carefully, thought he had done well by himself, his subject, and presumably his students, only to discover that only three students registered for the course when he repeated it. We all know such occurrences. The trouble is not that only three students registered, but that the professor had no hint that this would happen until registration day. However large or small that class, the students and the teacher were in no important sense face to face. The professor might as well have been talking to a television camera, with no audience at the receiving end.

There are scores of reasons for anxiety about the present threats to college education, not only in university systems that have two thousand acres of campus, but in colleges of five hundred, or one thousand, or ten thousand students. One of the anxieties has to do with how a relatively small company of teachers will teach a tremendous population of students. We meet this by exploring all the possibilities of using mechanical devices, and these will come to serve the purposes they can serve more effectively as we learn more how to use them.

One sign of this anxiety is the mounting body of research into learning by lectures, by discussion, by independent study, by teaching machines and television, whether students learn more if they do have direct communication with teachers than they learn without it. This is no place for a review of this research. There is some evidence that students who attend a class with five hundred students in a particular subject get as good grades on examinations in that subject as students who attend a class of twenty. Such evidence is easy to come by, and the obvious judgment easy to make. Whether or not this is a criterion of successful teaching by the teacher, or significant learning by the student is a more complicated judgment to come by. In a university lecture theatre, a walk around the back of the room, high up above the lecture platform, on the afternoon of a World's Series game, revealed the last five rows of students busy exclusively with their transistor radios; and if we contrast this with the scene around a seminar table where all the students were engaged in serious discussion, we come to another conclusion.

The bibliography of a single chapter on "Procedures and Techniques of Teaching" in *The American College* lists over 140 research studies on that subject completed between 1950 and 1960. Deans and department heads address themselves to the problem in dealing with faculty. A learned professor in a talk to young graduate-student teachers in a great university spoke of the difficulties of their apprenticeship, and went on to say:

> There are corresponding benefits; the beginning is more exciting than any other stage; your first promotion will exalt you as no other will; and you will have a direct and vital relationship with your students that will inevitably disappear, for freshmen are always the same age, and you will not be. The greater freedom and independence and dignity that will come to you as you journey and as you master, your growing sense of your command of your subject and of your ignorance of your subject — these will be well worth having. They must be paid for, however, with the realization of the increasing inability to reach the younger students, or, indeed, the great mass of students.

Such advice, certainly friendly enough, starts young teachers on their teaching road with the expectation that as they become older, wiser, and more understanding, they become less able to reach the freshman, can leave the freshmen to the new young assistants, and can themselves graduate to teaching graduate students. It is an accepted, built-in, and unfortunate impoverishment in the teaching of undergraduates that the profession has come to accept.

But the reason for writing about teaching here is that in every interview of an hour or two I had with students, they talked about their experience with teachers and teaching. For these students the association was crucial. During the period of intensive research into student attitudes, in the 1950s, a characteristic image of the student emerged. It describes him as detached, wishing to protect himself from association with teachers; and faculty, even in the more humane places, wishing to protect themselves from the students. In a discussion among men involved in such studies a distinguished college was described in this fashion:

> . . . the faculty has relations with students only in formalized ways. The tutors who are youngest and least experienced have the most difficult job — they have to relate to students. . . . Many faculty members feel that students make too many demands. If the pattern of hanging around chatting with students gets started, the faculty feels that time will be less their own.

And a professor talking with a colleague about the need to escape the students said, "Well, the first thing is to stay away from the coffee shop — I never go near it."

Riesman comments on the effect of such barriers, whoever erects them:

> In a large institution, as in a large department, it is almost inevitable that the faculty will be perceived as "them" whether or not the students develop the attitude of GIs or factory workers that "we don't have to take anything from them" and develop ways of punishing the rate-buster or brown-noser. Faculty members may in turn be prisoners of their peers; if they are (in Merton's terms) "cosmopolitans" they may feel unable to come to terms with the student culture as they interpret it, for they would regard this as sacrificing the strict demands of their discipline to the temptations of popularity and the compromises of an inferior institution.

A survey of students in a small, selective college with one of the highest ratios of faculty to students in the country shows that few students have frequent contact with their faculty. Most of them have little or none. When students were asked how many times they had contact with a faculty member outside of class, in the course of a year, the sophomores said three times, the juniors and seniors six times, on matters relating to their work. On matters of interest to them outside their work the sophomores said once, and the juniors and seniors twice.

The conclusion reached by the directors of that survey, as reported to the students in the study, was this:

> We would tend to conclude that the highly touted camaraderie between student and professor does not actually "come off" in most cases; however, a fairly large number of you were able to break through the barriers that might have discouraged you to establish relationships with your teachers. . . . At least for some, then, the promise of the "small college" atmosphere was fully realized.

When the atmosphere is against any natural human intercourse between teachers and students, individual efforts can be awkward and frustrating. Jacob tells the story of a professor, "one of the best teachers I have witnessed in action," who gave his students an open, general invitation to come to his home on a Sunday evening:

> Few but A students turned up. Then when he told them rather permissively, "this is your party, talk about anything you please," he found they were completely tongue-tied. They could not engage in a friendly, informal discussion. Finally, they got down to talking about sex and at that point the party thoroughly degenerated and people went away. There was never any inclination on their part or on his to renew the experience.

The fact that only A students turned up does not mean, as he suggests, that the others were indifferent to the professor, or to his invitation, or to both. A C student might want very much to have some live association with a teacher, but without more encouragement than this occasion provided, he would be likely to assume that no teacher wanted to see *him*. And one can scarcely wonder that friendly, informal discussion did not flow when the students were confronted with the proposal that they could now talk about anything they pleased, because it was their party. Adults, greeted in this fashion, would probably laugh a host down — but these students couldn't afford to do that. Such social relations often sputter and die because there is nothing to sustain them in the normal life students and professors have together.

On the basis of this incident Jacob raises the question of:

> a hiatus *within* a good many students themselves, a hiatus between their intellectual life and other aspects of living; whether what we are witnessing is perhaps the developing of a clear separation between the mental process and the living process. Maybe the modern sophisticated student can handle living in two different worlds, unbothered by the necessity of integrating knowledge with decisions in his personal life.*

In the same spirit, Freedman says:

> The student culture provides order and comfort. It instructs in how to behave in various social situations, in what to think about all manner of issues, in how to deal with common problems and troublesome external influences. It even offers instruction in how to keep the faculty at a distance, how to bring pressure that will

* Philip Jacob, *Spotlight on the College Student,* American Council on Education, 1959. pp. 33–35.

insure that the faculty behaves in expected and therefore manageable ways. It permits pleasant association with faculty members but discourages genuine relationships of a kind that might challenge the basic values of students. Although many students say they would like greater opportunity to associate with the faculty, what they often have in mind is aid in the solution of practical problems rather than relationship on an adult basis.*

The embarrassment students often feel in relations with members of the faculty distresses them — perhaps more than it does the faculty. It conflicts with a desire to communicate with their teachers in some way that is not merely formal. Students count their repeated failures to integrate what they are learning in their classes with their attitudes and decisions about their lives as a chief cause of a sense of isolation; and a true relation with a teacher is often their chief way of rescue. And this wish is not, as a cynical observer described it, a wish for "psychiatric baby-sitters."

Students talked about individual teachers frequently and with feeling; and because we talked more about experiences they valued than those they did not, they spoke most often about the kinds of teacher and teaching that had been important to their lives in the college years.

There was a tough and relentless insistence in Anderson's teaching that finally made Alex Rovere know that nothing could take the place of thinking through a scientific problem — neither memory, nor going through motions, nor outside help. "He kept insisting, 'What is the problem asking you?' " Alex said, until Anderson's conviction that this must be discovered communicated itself to his student for whom, in turn, the inquiry became a necessity. But the student never doubted — never needed to doubt — Anderson's concern for him and the importance of his understanding the process of learning.

Students who are becoming educated do not accept willingly the experience of being ignored by teachers, or resign themselves to feeling that they are of no importance.

An independent and self-directed student said of her college:

> This is really two colleges — one is the official one, formal and conservative, the other is the unofficial one, in which faculty members have made it possible to do things the official college makes no provision for. They are there when you need them.

* Mervin Freedman, "The Passage Through College," *Journal of Social Issues,* 1956, Vol. XII, No. 4, pp. 16–17.

Good associations of the students in this book with members of the faculty were not based, often, in a professor's interest in involving himself in the student's personal problems, nor were they the kind of relation two adults can have with each other. In the best of such associations there is always the distance created precisely by the fact that the student is *not* quite an adult. The unique quality of association between a teacher and a college student is that a mature individual interested in intellectual matters associates with an individual in the process of developing an intellectual and personal life; and this relation is one in which intellectual matters are the occasion and first cause of the association. If the professor who had such an unhappy experience with his students in his home had established, before the event, any on-going relation with his students, the evening would not have been so drearily lost. Students wish to be taken seriously, and their response when they are, is deep and lasting. The range of needs and of possibilities is great.

The ways in which teachers affect seriously the education of their students are many; but however the teachers function in the classroom, whatever their style, their subject, their way of talking to the students or with them, what students remember, what reached the heart of their learning, what they cherished more than any other one thing, is the sense of shared experience with a teacher. They know the teacher is going through something when the students are; the students speak of this when it is happening, and often afterward, for the sense of communion lasts.

One Harvard student described, as others did, too, the trouble he had when he came, finding a place to be, a place to take hold, a place to feel some solidity in the kaleidoscopic world of the college. Like others, he talked of the image he had had of Harvard before he came — a place in which students lived and had a common life. The variety of people and activities, the impersonality, the fashion among students of not needing anybody, obliterated that distant image of Harvard. Like others he managed to find his roots in a freshman seminar — one taught by Dorothy Lee who knew how to keep her own sense of privacy without having to keep students at a distance. That year, the seminar, with the associations it led to, was his anchor.

By the time he was a junior he was no longer in such urgent need of personal support, but he was always aware of what the teaching he experienced, as well as what he learned, meant in his own education. He was studying with Erikson, Tillich, and Riesman:

I haven't talked with any of them except Riesman, who seems to know you whether he has talked with you or not. I've not talked much with him, either — I think he knows you because of the way he reads students' papers. I find I don't need now any personal connection with them. They are so aware of the personal and human needs of people, and so of my needs, that if they are personally remote, they are deep in the human issues that are bothering me and other people. They talk about these things with compassion and interest as well as knowledge — and so they are talking with us. I don't need them personally.

Anna Warren said, of the teachers who re-created her intellectual life that, though they differed in many ways, "they were all alike in having a passionate commitment not only to what they were teaching, but to life — and they communicated this to their students." Helen Lynd in philosophy, Bert Loewenberg in American history, Muriel Rukeyser in poetry shared with students their conviction that what they knew, what it meant for life, and how they felt, were all one experience; it was this that Anna Warren discovered, and it was this that made a student of her.

Sometimes students found in teachers a quality of impersonal communion peculiarly important to them. An able freshman came to his university with the same talent for science and the same unconsciously settled expectation of studying physics that Scott Hansen had for mathematics. He encountered that first year an eminent anthropologist who (unlike many eminent professors) taught the freshmen. He was a busy scholar whose enthusiasm for exploration fired the boy's imagination as no study of physical science had. The man's awareness of how important this was to the student led him to encourage him on a new road to follow — found work for him to do that used all the scientific talent that had originally turned him to physics, but invested his study with imagination and meaning.

Students are as quick to recognize the "impersonal" teacher who cares that his students become fully engaged in their work, as they are to resent impersonality that cuts them off from communication — an experience they have often and feel keenly. "He is interested in what he is doing — in his own work; he is not interested in us."

There is another kind of teacher who creates experiences important to students' education — men who are personally observant, conscious of particular students' needs, interested and imaginative, fertile with ideas about work that could be important for a given student. Such teachers turn even students who are pedestrian and limited when they come to college into lively and exploring students. Rosenau, at Douglass College was such a teacher to several students who had come with limited experience and limited ideas of what was possible for them. He engaged them in practical aspects of the working of governments, of foreign affairs and political structure. He helped them become involved in activities and projects that brought what he taught them in political science to immediate and dramatic life, started them moving under their own power, let them go as far as they would. Mitau at Macalester is another — who took pains to give shape and direction to the vague wish for service some students brought from religious and often provincial homes. Such teachers care about what becomes of their students, but their concern for their students is not limited by a wish to do something *for* them. There is important experience to be discovered, work to be done, a world to function in; and the education of the students, their growth to manhood, the personal enlargement education should bring, has a better chance of accomplishment if the teacher can forward the experience, reveal work to do, help them to find in study ways to function.

Certain of the students I talked with came from homes where there had been no knowledge of college education, and schools that had given them neither the wish for, nor the experience of, intellectual life, no direction — sometimes not even the awareness that one needed to find a way of life. Sometimes they were suspicious and defensive, having come to college because it might be a practical thing to do. Often they were bright, and they had manipulated their way through high school and had come determined to manipulate their way through college, and by that means escape the life their parents had.

There were such students at Monteith College, and there were teachers who accepted the conditions of their coming, and their attitudes; made demands, but took pains to break the barriers to communication which were much higher with these students than with many. In sometimes inarticulate and ungraceful language they explained what teaching had done for them:

> Through contact with people, I learned to understand myself more and to understand other people. And in dealings with a few instructors . . . I began, you know, to look into myself and to find out what it was I was doing in school, and to me this is really something; because if by coming here and finding out what I'm here for, what I want and what I want to do later on, I can get my bearings.

Here, you know, I've been able to talk and not be on the defensive — not putting on an act all the time. If I don't know something I can come out and show my ignorance, and to me this has been a big help, because most of the time in high school and other courses at the University, I act my way through rather than learn. That has enabled me to learn rather than act, and it's a big step forward....

And it wasn't until I got into personal contact with some of the instructors that I began to realize that learning was more than this, and learning was more important than this....

And I think the relationship between the instructor and the student in Monteith is conducive to this. It would be an accident, I think, if it happened anywhere else, because if a person isn't an individual who makes friends with instructors, or shies away from them, he'll never be induced to do really constructive thinking.

Few of the students here will follow in the footsteps of their teachers — the young anthropology student might, but most of them will not. They are not, in that sense, modeling themselves on their teachers; but they wanted most and valued most teachers who not only gave them knowledge, but who shared the experience of knowledge, who communicated their own intellectual vitality, their conviction of the worth of ideas and the importance of feeling, the sense of life. Such teachers met them face to face; and this is what students leaving childhood and becoming men ask of them.

PART TWO
Conditions of Commitment

IX

Profile of the College Student

The Students and the Aims of Education

ALL the students who are part of this story were intelligent enough to do good college work, and most of the time they did. They were not always intellectual enough to satisfy professors that any time spent discussing their education was well spent. One young professor in a distinguished college looked at the names of the students in his college who were on my list, and said, disdainfully, "Middlebrows!" I think he thought they would not serve as glowing-enough examples of the accomplishments of the college, as some others might. They probably wouldn't.

But it seemed to me that perhaps the young professor even in that institution needed to learn that middlebrows — by his standards — are exactly what he is teaching; it is a pleasing fantasy of many teachers that they are in the classroom primarily to teach highbrows — that is, young men like themselves. (This view, by the way, coincides with the remark of the Harvard student that Harvard professors like to teach people who will become Harvard professors.)

In any case, we must take the consequences of having decided (a long time ago) that millions instead of hundreds of boys and girls would go to college, and study, between the ages of seventeen and twenty-one, something that is intended to make them better adults. Obviously a great many of them will be middlebrows in the young professor's sense — including some very bright ones. Certainly they will not become college professors, or specialists in the professor's field. The educational question is whether they will be thinking, humane, intelligently acting middlebrows or merely money-making, or merely country-club, or generally impervious ones.

The students in this book are variously gifted. None of them are geniuses, nor their education the education of geniuses. They are not the rare original scholars; not the artists; not the men who will make literary discoveries like the discovery of the metaphysical poets who had been lost in the libraries for nearly two hundred years; not the most truly seminal thinkers; not the men who will put known things together in ways no one thought of putting them together. Those are the special people to whom — one hopes — American universities will give an education that lives up to their abilities. Any one of the people in this book may some day turn out to be a special one, too. But that is not why they are here.

Rather they represent the millions whom America has now chosen to send to college, and when we fail to educate them it is a large failure, and as tragic, too, as failing to provide adequately for the education of the special ones. The students in this book, by the time they finished college, were making creative use of their education. Since they could not have done so without a commitment to their studies — a real effort to make something of them — it may be in order to consider some of the conditions of their commitment.

Some college students are more conscious than others but, aware or not, they are all engaged in a double effort — to understand themselves and their own natures, and their possibilities for learning and action; and to discover how to understand and cope with the tremendous changes taking place in the world around them. If what they learn, and how they learn, in college, does not further this effort, the function of the undergraduate college is poor indeed. In some terms, on some level, whatever vocabulary they use, this is what students are looking for.

What part does the formal education provided in an undergraduate college have in furthering this purpose? A great many people, just now, would like to simplify the responsibilities of the college by distinguishing between education and instruction, and they urge that we leave education — the development of the individual, the growth of the boy into a man — to the home, the church, the state, all the continuing forces that impinge on his life, and leave instruction to the college.

At a conference of educators called to discuss *The American College,** a distinguished administrator raised this as a major question. Commenting on the book he said:

* *The American College,* Nevitt Sanford, ed., New York, N.Y. John Wiley & Sons, Inc., 1962. This massive analysis of higher education is the work of more than thirty scholars—educators who are also philosophers, anthropologists, psychologists, sociologists. The studies of which it is composed in turn draw on the work of over a thousand others. It explores an enormous range of important ideas and experience in education.

I think that I detect in many of the contributors to the present volume a predilection toward making our colleges into institutions for personal and social development. Why should not other institutions of society perform those functions? Why should colleges not specialize in the promulgation of knowledge but leave to family, church, state, etc., the development of social and emotional life? The organization of a college faculty or curriculum need not permit it to improve the students' chances of voting soundly, preserving their marriages, or avoiding neuroses. Let us proceed with our research but restrain our missionary impulses.

The effort to make such distinctions gets us out of no dilemma at all. To instruct an engineering student in the physics he must know in order to understand stress in bridges means to give the information he needs if he is to build a bridge or design one. Instruction of that same student in the meaning of the *Phaedo,* or an understanding of *A Valediction Forbidding Mourning,* must involve his capacity for feeling, his values, his love — or what he learns means little or nothing. Instruction of that same student in the vast implications of modern physics for human life and human institutions should engage his mind, and his moral and social values, and should affect his way of growing from a child to a man. In those possessions of the mind that enter into what we call liberal education — those things that humanize and enlarge the spirit — there is no serious learning, no "instruction," without deep involvement of the person, his feelings, and his beliefs.

To say that a college or university has no function to perform in the student's developing life except to pass on traditional and useful forms of knowledge, is to ignore an inescapable function that will be served whether we recognize we serve it or not.

Whether a teacher pays any attention to a student's intellectual, personal, social, emotional concerns or not, he is involved with them. A student's response to poetry, his capacity to deal with social issues, his choice of a college major, his choice of a vocation, if these are serious experiences, must be deeply affected by the circumstances of his personal life and of the world he is growing up in. How much we can do about these circumstances, or their effect upon his learning, depends on the willingness of the institution (or of teachers in it) to recognize this educational purpose.

One of the reasons it is immensely difficult to know what makes education important to the life of a student is precisely that it is inseparably bound up with his personal needs and with the pressures of the world he lives in, on and off the campus. Evidence of this emerges in conversations with every student, in whatever kind of college, who cares to discuss his college life seriously. There is much evidence in both the full and the brief accounts of students in this book.

And sometimes this mingling of forces takes strange forms. Students are spurred to high endeavor as well as plunged into failure by their feelings. These feelings may have to do with occurrences that belong to the normal cycle of life, or with accidental or occasional circumstances. A boy, then getting ready to go to graduate school to study classics, explained his shift from English to classics by the catastrophic effect of his mother's sudden death. It first paralyzed him so he could do no work, he said, and then filled him with guilt for having dawdled his way through his classes, in both high school and college, taking the courses that were easiest, and getting by. Studying Latin and Greek meant to him accepting the kind of discipline he had always avoided, and, spurred by his remorse, he turned himself into a student of high achievement in a demanding field; a successful student of the kind colleges like to have. This, at least, is his explanation of a sudden plunge into study. His sense of guilt may turn him into a scholar, he may recover from the trauma and become a scholar anyhow, or the shock may pass and with it the intellectual drive.

No amount of curriculum-making or testing programs alters the fact that what students study, what they learn, what they think, if it is worth the time of a teacher to teach, an administrator to administer, a custodian to keep the corridors in order, will cut deep into the process by which a learning youth becomes a functioning adult, and the way he lives and acts in the tremendous drama of these times.

THE IMMEDIATE CONTEXT OF THEIR EDUCATION

The students in this book were born about 1938. They entered adolescence in the years after World War II. They entered high school the year the Supreme Court declared that racial segregation in public schools was unconstitutional, and belatedly the issue began to change the face and temper of college campuses.

Their high school and college years saw outside this country the emergence of new nations, and of millions of people on the continents of Asia and Africa whose existence had meant nothing whatever in the education of most of the teachers who taught these students. Suddenly teachers and students alike not only were confronted with the need to know what was taking place, but were soon forced to think about the impact of these events on what we know about learning, intelligence, race, political organization, character, social relations, personality, and communication between individuals.

Their college years were spent in a period of scientific advance which changed for everyone the face of the physical world.

The early 1950's, when they were in high school, witnessed in this country hysterical political attacks, which lasted into their college years, and distorted and disrupted the lives of hundreds of citizens, including teachers of the students in this book and the students themselves.

These were years of intense and vocal public interest in education at all levels — legitimate and illegitimate kinds of interest — a time of anxiety and dismay about our inadequacies; anxiety rooted in fear of the rising peoples of the world, of alien political systems, of the disastrous possibilities of nuclear war. Among all the other overturnings of our behavior, education, perhaps for the first time in history, became front-page news. More and more students were entering and preparing to enter college; and they were entering a world filled with greater dangers, and open to greater possibilities than at any time in history.

In the midst of both the public criticism of education and the political attacks that reached into the heart of most schools and colleges, including those that were the educational leaders in the country, there was also great self-exploration going on. During the 1950's an immense amount of educational research was trying to discover what was, indeed, the impact of liberal education on the attitudes and values of the rapidly growing proportion of young people who were spending the questioning years in college. The result of this research, conducted against the tumultuous events of the time, raised frightening questions in the mind of anyone committed to the cause of education in a democracy. What, indeed, *were* we accomplishing in those years?

THE SEARCH FOR ATTACHMENTS

This research repeatedly revealed that, in a time of tremendous excitement and change, college students — the intellectually superior, the socially favored young people of this society — were making their way through the college years, indifferent alike to the intellectual challenges of college itself, and to the social challenge of the historical moment.

By and large, college students were described by those who assembled great quantities of evidence about them, as coming to college, performing the tasks required of them, passing through college and out into their individual lives having felt little the impact of the values and ideals of the liberal education they presumably came there to get, or of the world it interprets:

> If one important function of a college is to induce students to re-examine their established ways and accepted habits of thought, it appears that the difficulties in the way of carrying out this function with the present group of students are great.*

Indeed some of the most impressive evidence of the failure of education to influence students' intellectual or moral values, to enlarge their humanity, comes out of the most privileged colleges. This evidence began to appear in the middle fifties — the year 1956 was one of dark revelation about students in our best colleges, revelations calculated to dismay anyone who had committed his life to teaching students.

That was the year Philip Jacob's *Changing Values in College* marshalled evidence collected by many people, demonstrating that there was little reason for teachers to expect to change students' values in college by their efforts as teachers — a suggestion that angered the dedicated, dismayed the hopeful, and confirmed the cynical with its image of students who were "gloriously contented" with the way they were, and had no inclination to permit education to make them into something else.

Not only the examination of students' use of their education in large institutions with mixed populations, but penetrating studies of the lives of students in the most highly favored and selective colleges drew the same conclusions, painted the same pictures of the contemporary student. One must do the work required of one, but not too well; faculty are not to be allowed to affect one's life; when a student steps out of line, whether by behaving too badly, or studying too much, or becoming too interested in controversial issues, fellow students have ways of bringing him into line. Students create a private world that exists alongside and largely independent of the academic world of the college — the world in which the college intends students should have their principal life. That year it was said of Vassar students that:

> Except for a minority, the fundamental philosophy of the college and its academic and intellectual aims do not enter primarily

* Mervin Freedman, *op. cit.,* p. 18.

into the formation of the central values and habits of life of the student body. Instead, for most students, educational experiences are assimilated to a central core of values and dispositions which is relatively independent of the more formal academic influences.*

In the same year, James Davie and Paul Hare reported in a piece called "Button-Down Collar Culture," on their research at an Ivy League university. Here, too, it is important to be "well-rounded," which means, for one thing, that one must not become too much involved in intellectual matters, one must study, but not too much; not be seriously engaged in exploring ideas or in concern with debatable issues:

> The theme of well-roundedness asserts pressure on the student to spend his time on other than intellectual activities once his continued existence has been assured by the meeting of minimal requirements. . . .
> Once they feel secure in this respect, one finds increasing concern for the informal standards of the peer group. By sophomore year, one finds more mention of "the system" and "curve-wreckers." This implies that there is a general tendency for the student to have learned what the formal standards are, and exactly what amount of work is necessary to get certain grades.†

Of genuine intellectual interest there is little evidence.

These studies, and others as well, suggest that at a time of great upheaval many students, even in the selective and sought-after colleges, found ways of quite escaping the lively and probing intellectual life such colleges expect to provide. Other studies of more mixed populations project the same picture.

Nor were these studies of the middle fifties the end. A dozen others since then tell the same story of the failure of education to be more than casually important to students. In 1962, when these students were entering their last year, or were graduating from college, Kenneth Keniston drew a dismal picture based on "observations over the past decade of a number of able students in an 'elite' college."‡

He points out — and anyone would have to agree — that, in the processes of social change, "most affected are youths in the process of making a lifelong commitment to the future. . . . it is youth that must

* "The Passage Through College," *Journal of Social Issues,* 1956, Vol. XII, No. 4, p. 15.
† "Button-Down Collar Culture: A Study of Undergraduate Life," *Human Organization,* 1956, Vol. 14, No. 4.
‡ "Social Change and Youth in America," *Daedalus,* Winter, 1962, pp. 154–60.

chiefly cope with the strains of social change." He believes that "elite" youth feel these strains most acutely. What happens in academic life itself is without power to help them cope with these strains, and so they retreat.

The college student, Keniston says, is adrift. There is among students a feeling of powerlessness — it is a world the individual cannot control, or shape, or design — even the small part of it in which he lives. Borrowing Riesman's language, he speaks of the "privatism" of young men and women, which causes them increasingly to "emphasize and value precisely those areas of their lives which are least involved in the wider society, and which therefore seem most manageable and controllable." He speaks of the disinclination to undertake long-range endeavors and commitments; and the concern with what is private and present leads to "the decline in political involvement . . . a pattern of political disengagement."

I was not searching out these unrooted and disengaged young men; but on several occasions they sought me out. In them I found, even more disconcerting than their sense of drift, a strong wish not to be adrift.

Four students called one noon, having heard I was visiting their campus, and talking — as they put it — with students who liked what they were getting in the college.

"Your sample is biased," they said.

I knew it was no sample, and that it was biased.

"We think you should know what it is like on the other side of the tracks."

They talked about the other side of the tracks for two hours over lunch in a dining hall, contemporary and severely elegant, in a distinguished college which admitted only students with minds good enough to do academic work of high quality. It was in 1962 and they were nearing the end of their junior year. There were two gloomy hours of talk. One had dropped out of college at the end of his freshman year, and had now returned. He had wandered through that first year:

> scared the whole time. I was sure I couldn't make the grade, and when I found I'd done it, I didn't know what I'd done it for. I thought if I got out and saw the country that might help — and this place might look good to me.

He hitchhiked across the country and back, took jobs, supported himself, came back to college:

I wasn't so scared any more; I knew I could do it, but I still don't know why I'm here. What do you get out of this kind of education anyhow?

It was so with two others. The fourth had chosen to go to medical school as the least undesirable among the life choices that presented themselves, and was waiting it out until he could get his degree and leave the college. He had sought out a medical school on the other side of the country; he thought geography might make a difference. All of them were passing courses with good grades, but whatever the college thought, they knew education was a failure, and they felt the failure deeply.

Again, in "The Button-down Collar Culture" the not-surprising finding is reported that "the most meaningful contacts some students have with college authority figures are with the athletic personnel"; and this is put down by the researchers as evidence that the non-intellectual values are more important to the students and have more influence than the intellectual ones, because:

> given a person who is a product of American culture, where the professional athlete is more prestigeful than the professional intellect, and introducing that person to the college scene, it is not surprising that his tendency toward anti-intellectualism does not disappear or often not even noticeably diminish.

There is another, simpler explanation for the influence of the coach than the high regard in which Americans hold athletes. Often the athletic coach is the only person who talks to students as though they were human beings, who knows more about them as individuals, and has more interest in them as individuals, than the academic dean or the faculty who teach them. It isn't beneath his dignity to talk to them about what they need to talk about, as it often is with faculty members.

Fraternities have been a powerful force in capturing students and giving them a sense of belonging; if no sense of purpose. Comparing the life of a freshman in a fraternity-bound middle-western university with the life he found as a student at Harvard, Robert Brown wrote:

> For the incoming freshman no task is as difficult or as important as getting a bid to the "right" fraternity. His status for the rest of his college career will depend on his success in impressing upperclassmen during the week of rushing. Although rushing lasts a week, most of the freshmen had pledged by the third day, several on the first.

A "big brother," assigned by the fraternity is there for advice:

> and usually assistance, with dating, academic, and other problems.
> In some cases this relationship can assume a perfunctory warmth,
> in others, certainly, a meaningful friendship develops.
>
> It is obvious that the fraternity system artificially divides the
> freshman class. . . .
>
> The freshman has no time for members of other fraternities. No
> doubt this deprives him of valuable opportunities to form friend-
> ships. On the other hand, confronted by the enforced friends of
> the pledge class, the freshman will be able to re-examine and, if
> need be, alter . . . an identity he formed in high school. The en-
> forced fraternity unity of the freshman year gives way to what
> may be only perfunctory unity in the junior and senior years, and
> allows the individual to seek out his friends where and with whom
> he pleases. We must not forget, however, that during the first two
> years there are some . . . who have internalized values which dis-
> criminate against certain races, religions, and even low prestige
> fraternities. . . .
>
> In summary — he will rate himself and others as his fraternity
> is rated. He will be conscious of the fraternity in all his activities.
> . . . it will be particularly difficult to do anything that runs counter
> to the fraternity system of values.

The Harvard student, he said, escapes the "forced unity" of a
fraternity, but may find no allegiance to take its place:

> Dining seems the one very important exception to a rule of iso-
> lation. Breakfast is generally a lost cause, but lunch and dinner
> are the principal meeting place for the house members. . . . There
> are, of course, other meeting places available to individuals. Ac-
> tivities, offices, Cronin's, and clubs, all provide outlets. But one
> can drink, eat, play pool or build stage props only so much of the
> time and only by consciously, except for eating, setting out to do
> them.
>
> Harvard cannot escape its reputation as the finest school in the
> country. As such it attracts, according to "Information for Pros-
> pective Students," an extraordinarily diverse, able, and lively
> group. . . . At Harvard "there is help if you ask for it," but asking
> for help implies that one cannot meet competition. . . .
>
> > Lonely, lonely men of Harvard,
> > Set apart from all the rest;
> > Lonely, lonely men of Harvard,
> > Just because you are the best.

Stephen Sands spent a year out of school before entering Harvard.
He was startled, he said, by the "undifferentiated mass" that Harvard
seemed to be when he came as a stranger:

I found then that there isn't one Harvard. There are a great many, and if you are to have some anchor here, some place to move from, people to move with, you have to find your own Harvard. A boy comes here and he decides that he has to commit himself to something. So he shuts out everything else, and plunges — he might plunge into athletics or into work in the library, or the theatre, or on the paper or one of the social clubs, and that becomes Harvard for him and everything else is shut out.

Students find other ways, without the help of the college, to resolve their doubts and discover directions. A number of students like the unhappy one who wandered around for a year out of college and then returned still a wanderer, drop out and return; sometimes with much greater profit than he.

A pre-medical student, then a senior, said he had taken a year out after a rootless sophomore year:

I had always rather taken for granted that I would study medicine; I liked the kind of study it required, and I could do well. But I found I wasn't sure.

One thing that made him not sure was that he had some talent for sculpture, and a persisting wish that he might be a sculptor. So he dropped out of college for a year and became an apprentice to a distinguished sculptor. The artist worked mainly in metal, and the student learned how to weld, how to handle metal; he watched the daily work of the sculptor, and had place and time to work himself. At the end of the year he returned to the college:

I discovered in that studio the difference between being an amateur and being a professional. He is a professional in the best sense. I haven't it in me to become a professional of the sort he is. I learned that. I do have it in me to be a good doctor — maybe a very good one — that kind of professional.

Most of the students I talked with had found, by the time I met them, in their third year at college, a way to cope with isolation, had found a way of living and working in the college. For them, their work had become an anchor — but the effort, the failure, or the success in their search to make alliances, to find some base, to belong somewhere, was for many of them the part of their early college years they remembered most vividly and poignantly. "You *have to* belong somewhere before you can be something or do something" — it was a boy who came from a home and a life alien to everything in the intellectual life of the college, who said this need was a cause of his own deepest anxiety.

Karen Duncan had been an honor student in high school, and as a junior she was working well. But she described a painful beginning. Coming to an urban college she found herself isolated, unable to do her work, or even to know what she wanted to study. The help she got was formal and perfunctory. She spoke later of the misery of that first year. It took a long time to face the fact that she really was on her own, that nobody would bother with her. It took a long time, even, to find out the difference between work in the college and work in high school:

> There the discipline came from the outside, and the consequences were quick and clear. Here nobody knew or cared or made you do anything. I didn't have it in myself; I don't think I even had a self.

She took a typing job outside of college, working twenty-five hours a week. "They never knew about it." It was a way of flying from the work she couldn't do. It would be *something* done, anyhow. "I didn't even need the money."

Other students lived through such isolation. I was never convinced that surviving it strengthened character. Most often it seemed to me to have been a waste.

Obviously some students come to any college already committed to the intellectual life, ready to explore their own questions, asking only for independence and a chance to work in the relative freedom of the college. What they find to study suits their needs, the library is there for them to use, the faculty need make no special effort to induce them to take what they can. They grow up and become educated. Such a student is a natural for professors to teach, and for the college to educate. He makes his own connections with the parts of his environment that contribute to his education.

But there are a great many students in all colleges for whom this is not so. Observation reveals this, and the studies of students pile up evidence that too many of our students work casually, although often well enough so no one knows the difference; drift in the college, or drift out; make attachments that prevent them from involving themselves in their work. But so far the studies give us little indication of what professors, educational philosophers, courses or studies, do to cope with this condition.

The most comfortable response for educators to make to this picture of the college student, detached, or lonely, without serious involvement in work, is that he is a casualty of a dislocated world in which he sees no hope for himself; it is in this context he is most often described. This abdication comes easy; and the trouble may indeed go beyond the reach of education. But the evidence is that we do not often try. We continue to encourage students to come to college, and we continue to teach them. They come in larger and larger numbers, we raise higher and higher hurdles, design more and more cunning tests for the competitions that will decide who stays out, who comes in. We will not strengthen the meaning of college for students by these means or their ability to cope with the dislocation of the times, although we may get more and more intelligent students, and students who in one sense are "better prepared" for college.

We cannot cure in the college the illnesses of the time. But on the whole we make too little effort to discover how the knowledge of history and of the present, of personality and the cultures of peoples, the physical world itself — resources at the command of no other institution as fully as they are at the command of the college — can be used to combat withdrawal and indifference, and give students the chance, at least, to seek meaning and direction for their lives.

It is the purpose of the institution (a report of the Harvard freshman seminars says), to encourage a student:

> "to reflect on his beliefs and criticize his pre-suppositions," but too often that command goes unheeded or unheard — sometimes for four "creditable" years. On the other hand, when it *is* heeded, when the student begins to question his preconceptions and his definition of himself, he too often fails to find *in his intellectual experience in the college* place, encouragement, or materials for reconstruction.

I have recorded below some of the ways in which place, encouragement, and materials for reconstruction were provided for the students in this book.

X

When the Curriculum Encourages Attachment

WHAT students experience when they first come to college is crucial. The first year, indeed the first months, can be a revelation, a grim disillusionment, or just another routine stage to be endured. Some students spoke of how imagination was kindled at the very beginning — and how that made all the difference. A good many look back on that year with distaste and resentment.

They remember three kinds of freshman year — which they describe variously but vividly:

> Well, it was repeat and review, mostly.

> They piled it on; and we sank or swam — I swam, luckily.

> It was like an explosion in my life — I never thought so much or thought I could possibly be so absorbed.

Even colleges, reviewing their own behavior, recognize these three kinds of freshman year:

> Many students expressed dissatisfaction with their course work which was pictured as unstimulating and repetitious of their secondary school work.

> During their first year at college the freshmen had undergone their "ordeal by fire."

> It was to be an experiment that somehow would ignite curiosity, encourage commitment, command honesty.

As the high schools send on students for whom they are now providing intensified and fast-paced years, the hazards of a "repeat and review" freshman year at college become greater. The educational values and the problems of the year that "piles it on" have to be reconsidered, too. More students are coming to college from high school years that piled it on; and if some of them are therefore readier for intellectual adventure, it is already clear that some of them bring a kind of anxious acquisitiveness about learning that needs more than ever a freshman year that will not be an ordeal by fire, but will instead ignite curiosity, encourage commitment, and command honesty.

A study made by a college that admits only students with high school averages well in the eighties reports that more than three quarters of a recently graduated class were critical of the kind of freshman year they had had. They talked of:

> The poor quality of teaching in the basic courses where there is greatest need for motivating an interest in the subject matter. Several even claimed that teachers made no secret of being bored and dissatisfied with the required courses they were assigned to teach.

These students were not alarmed at the high standards, or the amount of work they were asked to do. Their complaints had to do with the unwieldy size of classes and the poor teaching that first year:

> Part of the student criticism of instructors and courses included dissatisfaction with poor textbooks, vague assignments, overemphasis on grades and, in general, poor planning by instructors.

An exhaustive research study in a distinguished private college reports on students' satisfactions and dissatisfactions with their first year. A third of the troubles they had refer directly to academic matters — others do by implication. Many of these describe the year as a "boring repetition of senior year at prep school"; "poor teachers in poor required courses"; "tremendous amount of repeat work."

A student poll in a small liberal arts college, where morale is high among both teachers and students, and where there is great respect for scholarship and commitment to teaching — even here students' criticism of the teaching in the first two years is sharp. Indeed their only serious complaint of the college was with:

> the quality and method of teaching during the first half of the college curriculum. This is especially significant . . . for then the quality of a course is more important than its particular subject.

Such inquiries, whether by students or research teams or a self-examining faculty, repeat these problems frequently enough to make it obvious that too often colleges simply do not do what is needed to engage the minds and hearts of students for learning.

Reports on the freshman year in some colleges assume that it is, and must be, a time of travail and anxiety:

> During their first year the freshmen had undergone their "ordeal by fire" and most of them had successfully completed the transition between high school and college. Probably their most valuable experiences for the future had been the realization that they

had to assume responsibility for their accomplishments and that success at college demanded concentration on studies and wide-ranging intellectual curiosity. It must be admitted that the whole problem of student "complaints" remains a puzzle. It may indeed be true that both high school counseling and college freshman counseling leave much room for improvement. . . . But the puzzle remains how to distinguish between character spinelessness on the one hand and, on the other, the "natural," so to speak, perturbation of the student who sees with more or less clarity that his despondency is itself a challenge of college and of the promise of success in life awaiting him after his college days are completed; that the urgency of the new need to rigorous self-examination, intellectually and in terms of character, is precisely what college is all about.

And it is argued that perhaps this suffering is a good thing — indeed that "perhaps even more severe measures should be adopted to compel a more thorough self-examination on the part of each student." And a caution is expressed lest we sentimentalize the student's need, and thus "cripple the student (and the citizen later) instead of aiding him":

> Happily . . . the freshman student in a significant number of cases does grow up, and a survival of the fittest does take place with or without extensive counseling aid.

The assumption behind this freshman philosophy is that the fittest do survive — that those who do are the best students for us to go on with; and that those who fail are no serious loss. Unfortunately there is a great deal of evidence that this is not necessarily the case.

Colleges discover that one way students adapt to a freshman year, when they cannot attach themselves to their studies, is to enter a life protected by the "student culture." Observations of freshmen in a carefully selected college population tell us that:

> The freshman year determines the basic orientation to the college and goes a long way toward either establishing or reaffirming certain enduring habits and values of life. For the great majority of students it is a happy year. Almost all adjust successfully to the peer society and find appropriate companionship, at least one or several students, if not many, with whom they can share thoughts and feelings, in whom they can find support. Those who are not quite prepared on arrival for the high level of work expected of them may have a difficult time academically, but social satisfactions often offset this strain. Within a short time freshmen are

caught up in the relatively self-sufficient student culture; family ties are attenuated, extra-college pressures are minimal, real faculty influence is yet to come.

Social satisfactions often offset the strain; *real faculty influence is yet to come,* but, it is also said, *the freshman year determines the basic orientation to the college.* Good students, who did find in their college education the intellectual and personal enlargement we look for when we undertake to educate them, were not satisfied to substitute social satisfactions for academic ones, nor satisfied with such postponement of faculty influence. Unless they have become indifferent to the whole matter, by the time they are juniors or seniors they look back with regret and indeed speak often quite bitterly of a freshman year that failed to be the vital experience they had come there to find. Able students getting ready for graduate school said:

> The real challenge came, to begin with, from things I did outside my courses. I was interested in writing — wanted very badly to write — but the freshman English course had a syllabus we had to follow, and I hadn't a chance for any voice in what I might try writing. It was very hard, that freshman year. I had been good at math, but I found the math course incomprehensible, and I couldn't get any help. I kept a record of my working hours as a freshman and found I was doing over sixty hours of work a week. The history course was dull, but I thought I had to stay there, because a student is expected to work with whatever teacher is assigned — so I spent five hours on each assignment to make up for the loss in the classroom.

> . . . .

> There was nothing new, that freshman year, in what we were given to study. The new things were my own thoughts, my trying to place myself. New things to study came after the first year.

> . . . .

> The English composition course was unbelievably boring — we needed to have practice in writing, because we all had a lot to learn — but nothing much happened. Students come into college excited, and then in the second month or so it disappears. This is sometimes because of social trouble; or some of the students don't know how to study as they are expected to study here; and there is a great deal of disillusionment because of dull freshman classes. In the big general courses an enormous lot of material is crammed in, and what the lecturer wanted was to get his own opinions back. If you were good at that you were a good student.

Some of the cannier ones had found ways of escaping at least part of a dull freshman program:

> I live near the university, so I went to summer school before my freshman year and got off a couple of dreary courses — basic they call them.

.   .   .   .

> Luckily I escaped the boredom of the freshman year, by talking my way out of some of the mammoth freshman lecture courses. I actually had a chance to talk with a professor before my junior year, that way.

Experimental Freshman Years

THREE of the colleges in which I interviewed students had created new and imaginative programs for their freshmen. They are not honors programs, and they are for different kinds of students. Harvard freshmen come from good private or public schools, have high entrance scores, have lived in homes with college-educated parents most of whom live comfortable business and professional lives. The freshmen of The New College, a small experimental college related to Hofstra University, come from middle-class suburban homes, not wealthy, but not poor, whose parents have sometimes gone to college, sometimes not. Their fathers are small businessmen, technicians, perhaps superior building custodians, sometimes accountants, occasionally lawyers or dentists. Monteith College, attached to Wayne University, in Detroit, draws freshmen from lower- and lower-middle-class industrial homes. Their fathers are workers in the auto plants, taxi drivers, construction workers. Many of these young people are the first generation in their families born in this country.

All three programs demonstrate that the educational purposes in such diverse institutions may be identical, although, when attention is paid to the particular needs of the students to be taught, the content or organization of the work may differ widely. They also demonstrate that it is possible in a public institution, a non-privileged private institution, and a highly selective institution alike, to design creative and exciting educational programs that at the very beginning capture the energies and imagination of the students. There is a good deal of talk about the sub-cultures in colleges, and how these interfere with education. These special programs or "satellite" colleges have created powerful sub-cultures that advance the purposes of education instead of hindering them. The programs are independent enough to permit the faculty to work in quite different ways from the ways of the parent institution. They can proceed with their work without disturbing the work of the rest of the university, or even its equilibrium. They are all looked on with skeptical eyes by the more orthodox in the parent establishment, and they all proceed about their business nevertheless.

Students who have had freshman years in these programs almost without exception recall with satisfaction the quality of its life and thought.

Attitudes toward freshmen determine what kind of freshman year is provided for students, and some of the learning-by-suffering attitudes have already been described. The aims and designs of these freshman studies were also determined by convictions about what beginning students need.

THE HARVARD FRESHMAN SEMINARS

Harvard, of the three places, could expect to have entering freshmen who were already on their intellectual way, and seminars were planned at first with such students in mind:

> We had at the start been very much concerned about the student who came to Harvard College with a strong and advanced interest in a particular field, who by his own initiative had got deeply involved in the concerns of that field, and who on coming to college found himself in courses that neither offered much depth nor asked initiative or involvement. We had seen cases where this experience not only had been hard on morale but had seriously undermined a potentially fast and durable engagement in the life of the university. By offering, in some seminars, opportunity to sustain that initiative and interest while simultaneously carrying on essential course work, we had hoped to capitalize more effectively the strengths of a great many incoming students.
>
> We were to some extent wrong. The evidence, in the first place, is that though the exceptions are very visible, relatively few students bring to Harvard such *commitment*.

.   .   .   .

> There have been students, of course, who have come with single-minded purpose and found in a seminar exercise for a professional preoccupation that had long since left behind questions of choice and commitment. And where they have known themselves well the opportunity has been invaluable. The physics student who wrote, almost arrogantly, that "I am definitely, for better or worse, a specialist. I have been for at least six and probably sixteen years, and I will continue to be one," knew himself adequately and is now on his way to a distinguished career in physics.

But most of the freshmen for whom we hoped to provide opportunity of this kind have been far less confident of their academic predispositions and have used the seminars less to sustain commitment than as a means of "checking it out."

It was the intention of the seminars:

to provide, vividly and early, a widely relevant introduction in depth to a significant area of study; to create "general ignition"; to afford the student opportunity to discover what the university is about and what his possibilities are within it. What seemed to be needed by many students . . . was a sense of engagement in the life of the university.

It was a purpose of the seminars to cope with the "culture shock," to provide for the student "in his intellectual experience in the college place, encouragement or materials for reconstruction." This need is expressed often by the students in their own way, as by the students who said:

I think there is a certain danger in taking an individual the way Harvard does, and I guess most of the colleges do, and throwing him into this huge threshing machine and cutting off all his roots and then there is nothing else that he has.

   .   .   .   .

It has not been the function of the seminars to *provide* self-confidence. They have sought rather to provide a setting in which the student might discover, intellectually, meaningful basis for confidence.

   .   .   .   .

He criticized without discouraging me — instead gave me great faith in myself and taught me that I could think.

A faculty member saw this function of the seminar in these terms:

My feelings based on my own seminar and experience with students in the seminar last year make it very clear that the freshman seminars have been a major force in saving a large number of students from a very total kind of apathy that one often finds in the undergraduate body at Harvard.

A report on these seminars, written after their first four years, pointed out that they differ greatly in style and content but concludes that "a few things can be said about the general characteristics that have had most to do with the seminars' shape and impact."

They have utilized inquiry in depth

> as a means of demonstrating the nature and methods of a signifi-
> cant academic area;

> to provide opportunity for the student to discover what scholarly
> inquiry in *general* is about — the kinds of competence and imag-
> ination and discipline and honesty it requires;

> as a means of taking the student quickly to a level of inquiry at
> which the interdependence of fields becomes clear and inescap-
> able; and

> to give early opportunity for the student to test strenuously his
> academic pre-dispositions.

They have sought, by associating the student in an intellectual context
closely with a member of the faculty and a small group of students

> to give live, close demonstration of the ways in which an educated
> mind approaches intellectual problems;

> to provide a mobile vehicle for pursuit of investigations;

> to make it possible to tailor instruction in such a way as to provide
> each student, and the group as a whole, maximum challenge;

> to encourage students to learn from each other; and

> to provide for self-examination and self-discovery a supportive
> context appropriate to the intellectual aims of the university.

> They have been voluntary and gradeless, and they have been inde-
> pendent in their identity, by and large, from field requirements
> and the departments.

How Scott Hansen used the seminar is a part of the history of his
education at Harvard. He was one of many.

Joe Steinberg talked about how his feeling about studying changed
that first year. He began by saying he had "lost the idealism" he had had
in high school. What he meant, he said, was that in high school everything was very easy for him, and doing what was expected was easy, too.
His grades were good, he was a promising student of science, and his
plan was to go to Harvard, and then to medical school.

At the time of this discussion he was a junior, recalling himself as
a freshman. In high school everybody and everything seemed good.

What his teachers said seemed right; and what his parents said seemed sound. Studying was satisfying, and one of the most satisfying things about it was that if you listened and followed directions you knew what you had to do, you did it, and you were finished. The rewards were there for doing what ought to be done, and it was not difficult to get the rewards. He felt confident about his relations to other people. He had a lot of ideas about what was right, and he could tell when people were wrong.

His freshman year unsettled his certainty about what he believed in, and it made him dissatisfied with the kind of studying he had done. He saw more possibilities, more dangers, he said — nothing seemed quite as clear as it had before. The feeling of uncertainty was very disturbing, but he said he started thinking about all the things in his life he had assumed were decided.

This is what discussions in the seminar began for him, and where he got started. This was not what most of those in authority at Harvard were looking for:

> Most of them are interested in having you arrive at ends and are not interested in the process of accomplishing them — not everybody, but almost everybody.
> The jobs the professors set you in making assignments require that you come back with certain kinds of information when they ask you for it — what really counts *with you* in what you read, what advances your own thinking, might be quite different — and these responses can remain entirely apart.

He spoke of the unity among the students in the seminar group in contrast to the isolation in most situations in the college, the competitiveness in work. Each man has to be getting on as far and as fast as he can himself. Here there was no sense of competition, and a community of understanding was established around books, and arguments, and ideas.

Students talked of how their attitude toward their work changed in the course of the year, and of new directions they found for study. A science student said he learned here how important it is for a scientist to be something more than a scientist; and another who thought he was headed toward mechanical or chemical engineering became interested in medicine, and began to think about whether he might consider going into medical research.

A good many students spoke of the importance of the seminar to an increased understanding of themselves, and of what learning can mean to them:

It has been much more than another course. It has been a living experience involving one's whole person — mental, spiritual, and emotional. This program has given me an inside view of the attitudes and beliefs of the university, and made me feel a sense of excitement and comaraderie which has been part of the seminar's activity.

THE NEW COLLEGE OF HOFSTRA

The New College is a special unit or "satellite" of Hofstra University on Long Island, and like its parent is designed for commuting students. It began as a program offering from one to two years of college credit, after which students were expected to transfer to Hofstra University, or, if they chose, to another institution.*

In this "intellectually challenging and cohesive academic year" students worked in only two courses at one time. One offered a broad, interrelated approach to science and the humanities, the other intensive study in a specific intellectual discipline.

The "Introduction to Science and the Humanities" continued throughout the year, and all students took it:

> During this course each teaching fellow presents the intellectual history, basic points of view, methods, and current problems of his discipline. Literature, physical science, fine arts, mathematics, philosophy, and social science are studied. Emphasis is on evaluation of evidence and ways of knowing.

Alex Rovere entered The New College in its first year. There were a hundred students and six faculty members, called Fellows — one in each of the disciplines.

Each student elected in addition an intensive course in one of the disciplines represented in the faculty, taking three such courses, in succession, during the year. These courses, each having fifteen to twenty students, met in the afternoons for class sessions, discussion groups, experiments, problem sessions, and study. The faculty member teaching the specialized course became the adviser of the students in that course, but all the Fellows came to know all the students in a friendly and engaged environment. This faculty ranged in age and experience from a young man in the process of completing his Ph.D. to a distin-

* The academic New College calendar was thirty-eight weeks long, permitting the student to earn extra credits during the regular year, and allowed time also for those who wanted to, to attend a summer session at the parent college. Acceleration was important for some students, but was not the main contribution of this program.

guished retired professor who took on the new assignment with all the zest of a youth he had never lost. On an anonymous questionnaire given students after they had left The New College for Hofstra more than 80 percent of the replies indicated that teacher-student and student-student relations had been the most valuable aspects of their experience at The New College. They valued next, in order, the "integration and continuity of the courses" and the "concentration in the morning course."

All the academic activities of the college were housed in a single building. Faculty offices, classrooms, and study rooms were within easy access of each other. It was no place for a professor to be who wanted to escape his students at the earliest possible moment.

The student comes to The New College from a different world than the Harvard student. He has been less well trained, and he is not fortified with such high academic scores. But The New College program, like the Harvard seminars, has been created to involve him as fully as possible from the beginning. This college has many students who have done only moderately well at school, their motivation in coming to college is sometimes both weak and suspect, they are often supported neither by the expectation of a family and the tradition of education and the superior high school education of the Harvard student, nor the upward-looking ambition of children of first-generation parents one finds at Monteith. These are children of small business men who look on college as a proper next step for their children. The ability is not unusually high, in most cases; and often, when they begin, the motivation for study is not very strong.

Leo Frank was such a student. He had gone to a Yeshiva high school, where they had kept after him every day, and, as he put it, "kept me going. I was always bored in school. I was not ready for what I found at New College, and I did badly in spite of help. I didn't know what it meant to work; and in the middle of the year they told me I would have to leave." He was determined to stay. "I knew there was something there I shouldn't lose — I started lobbying and they finally let me stay."

"He works hard, and he is a perfectionist," a teacher wrote, by the end of the first year, "but the boy has a rocky road."

At the end of the time there he went to another college. It was "a letdown." But he had come to look on learning with new eyes during that first year; a small group of students organized an informal seminar for reading and discussion, and his study of history became a serious pursuit in spite of the let-down. "I'm about a thousand years behind in the History of Western Civilization," he said, "because I started reading about the Greeks and buried myself in the stacks for a week when I should have been doing something else."

The open situation, the encouragement to ask questions, gave direction to this undisciplined boy, as it did to others, and a genuine intellectual life began which has now imposed its own discipline.

MONTEITH COLLEGE, WAYNE STATE UNIVERSITY

The Monteith College program includes studies in three large divisions of knowledge — a four-semester sequence of studies in the natural sciences, a three-semester sequence in the social sciences, and a three-semester sequence in the humanities. For the first two years, half a Monteith student's work is designed by the Monteith faculty, half is in the regular liberal arts college of Wayne University. The Monteith part is reduced to a quarter of his program in the third and fourth years. The Monteith freshman, like the Harvard Seminar freshman, does not have the experience of total immersion in the experimental program that The New College student has, but his identification with Monteith is strong.

In the Monteith courses half the student's time is spent in lectures and half in very small discussion groups. The relations established between the students and the faculty of the college as basic to the educational program, are described elsewhere. All the members of the staff participate in the lectures, individuals work with students in their particular areas.

This program and The New College program are organized quite differently in content; but many of the purposes are the same, and, as in the case of the Harvard Seminar program as well, they provide both organized and unorganized ways in which students escape the anonymity of the freshman year, have a chance to discuss ideas and information with their teachers, establish relationships that give them roots both in the institution and in the intellectual life created in it. From students comes repeated evidence that such arrangements are a powerful influence in attaching students to the purposes of the institution, and of education.

I speak here of the social science sequence as illustrating the way the Monteith program serves the new student because, in addition to its purpose in introducing students to the nature of the social sciences, the methods of studying man in society, and to certain crucial topics common to all the social sciences, it caused these students to look in a disciplined way at the life of the city in which they lived:

> Many social scientists are interested in how man learns, what makes him toe the line; many are curious about the formation of groups, large and small, their development and dissolution; many are interested in the ways that forms of language, of kinship, of economic systems have an impact on man's actions.

It was these areas of "overlap" that were to serve as the base for reading and for the direct experience so important as part of this program, and so appropriate for this student body.

Students read and discussed basic questions relating to man in society against a backdrop of experiment and observation in the industrial-city world in which they lived, and in which most of them had always lived.

Discussing whether they should choose for students' reading contemporary statements of the problems to be explored, or classical statements dealing with such issues, the faculty said:

> Our predilection was for the great statement, the article which opened up the question, rather than for the most recent exploration in the lode. We preferred to have a statement that was complex, that was aimed at a fundamental problem rather than to select the precise description or testing of a relatively minor point. Our reasons were that the students should see the ideas when written large in the enthusiasm of discovery, that they should sense the difficulties of forging a language to describe a new world.

Along with their reading, as a means to understanding what direct observation and analysis can also tell about the behavior of man in society, all the students engaged in field-research projects. But the function of such field studies goes beyond teaching them something about social science research methods. Perhaps for all students, certainly for these students who came out of the industrial life of Detroit "actual experience in field research [is used] to turn the students into men capable of looking deeply into a situation and of thinking independently and responsibly about it, thus becoming wiser and more scholarly."

Many colleges have "field work" or work programs, which seek to give students a view of life that in their ordinary existence they do not see. In this instance students were taught to look with new eyes at a section of the world in which they had always lived. "I was born in Detroit," one of them said, "but I never saw it before."

A student undertook to make a study of the police-community relations, particularly the policeman's conception of his role in the area of race relations, and he described his discoveries:

> I did a study of the Police Department and the NAACP. When I did it the first time I had got two levels — the actual information from patrolmen in the survey I had drawn up — the questionnaire — and another level, the first level, or the prime level (the highest level) from the heads of various precincts I talked to. I talked to a number of different lieutenants and sergeants who gave me their idea of how a police officer handles racial relationships, what the good police officer does, how he handles the situation and what is expected of him; and the questionnaire showed me another level, perhaps what is actually thought by the police officer himself, what he is doing, or how he thinks he should be doing these things. Mr. H. gave me a great deal of help in this.
>
> I read segments of *Street Corner Society* while I was doing this to see if perhaps I could find some relationship with what was going on in street corner society, and what was going on from the information I had gathered. With these two levels, it really didn't show much. I talked to Mr. H. and he told me that perhaps I should go still farther in, look a little deeper. I had a friend in the police department, he was a sergeant at the time, and I went and talked to him, and he gave me still a third level — the level of what one might say is actually being done, at least from one man's standpoint; it was quite interesting to note how the higher echelon would try to present one view to the public, the police officer tried to stick to this view, but breaks it down to still another level; and when an individual, possibly someone who knows what is going on, gives you the information that you are trying to get, the basic level of information, one finds still this third level that I was talking about. What he told me brought to mind the graft, the corruption, and things of this nature that the individual, the public, is not supposed to see or know about.

Another student reported:

> The Social Science course . . . leaves room to work by oneself, to think and dream and come up with one's own ideas. . . . This unlimited way is what is close to my own heart and I therefore speak of what impressed me most. I have learned to look not only at the other side of a problem, but also all the other sides, tops and bottoms. I no longer have to depend on others so much. . . . I am learning about many different things and ideas which I feel I would have lost had I not come here. I feel that with this type of education I will be able to go farther in life and I will be much happier.

The students in these three programs differed immensely from each other in many ways — their previous schooling, the homes they came from, their preparation for disciplined study, their expectations of life — they were part of the great variety of American college students. But they were close together in their response to efforts made to understand them, to the effort of teachers to reach and engage them.

Some Special Efforts

EDUCATION AWAY FROM THE CAMPUS

OFF-CAMPUS STUDY gave enormous stimulus to the work of some students. College students are more free-wheeling, more mobile, more aware and knowledgeable about the world outside the campus than they have ever been in the past. One of our chief complaints about the attitudes and behavior of college students is that they are detached from and indifferent to the world outside the campus; that they are reluctant to take responsibility, or learn to work as adults work.

One reason this is so is that often colleges do not exploit the possibilities for initiative by students or create situations in which they can undertake work that has emotional and intellectual meaning for them — we may need to remind ourselves that this is a condition for successful work by adults as well as by college students.

I have written earlier of the "animating principle" or life-style of a college that gives it character and stamps the education of the students who attend it. Off-campus study that is part of the life-style of a college is not new. Antioch and Bennington colleges have extended periods in which students are absent from the campus, working at jobs approved by the college, sometimes related to their academic studies, sometimes not. Field-work experiences extending from short periods to a semester or a year have been an integral part of the work of many students at Sarah Lawrence College — field work undertaken as part of an academic course carried at the same time, rather than in separate "work periods."

An important part of the way the Monteith faculty designed the program for its students, all of whom live in the city of Detroit, was to relate the work in the social sciences to the life of the city, when this could be done. In some places field work is designed to give students some direct knowledge of a world different from the one in which they live, and which their own lives do not touch. The field work undertaken by the Monteith students served, as the discussion of the Monteith freshman year indicates, to give them a wider context for understanding the very world in which they *had* lived.

Studying outside the campus, as part of regular undergraduate education is changing the character of their education for many students, and those I interviewed had had a variety of experiences. Obviously some were casual and insignificant (as study in a classroom sometimes is); but some of it had a tremendous importance in sharpening students' understanding of their academic studies. I have mentioned the SPAN program in Minnesota — a program of study and work in which about eight colleges and the university participate. This requires students to spend a summer of work and observation abroad in a situation allowing a good deal of exploration while they are actually there, but that is structured and controlled at this end, both before they go and after they come back. A year of study relevant to the place they expect to go and the work to be done precedes their going — and this study is part of their academic program. They must present a written report on their return, they must be available to speak to interested groups in the community, to use what they have learned for the instruction of other people. The report too is part of their academic record, for which they receive regular credit. This is both a group endeavor (because seminars regularly conducted the year before they go involve groups of students preparing for different but similar tasks) and an individual endeavor also, for in the end the value of the experience depends on the individual student who has it. I earlier mentioned the way this program fit the climate of Macalester College, which participates in it. For some of those students this experience accomplished something toward their study of the political emergence of African nations, for instance, that would have taken them much more than three months to study and understand had they stayed in the library at home — even if the relevant material had been at hand. One of these students was attached to a major political figure in Ghana for the months of her stay there, and followed events day by day that she saw leading to political crisis. "Most of the people I spent time with are in jail now," she said a few months later. But she also spent time with medicine men in villages, and spoke of their combination function as minister, doctor, psychiatrist. "I can't feel quite as exclusive about my own religion again," this religious and somewhat provincial girl said, "or about our feeling of superiority because we begin to understand the relation of religion and medicine and psychiatry."

Another of these students spent time with young people of the Christian Democratic movement in Italy trying to discover how much this was a mass movement of young people conscious of their need to take part in their future, and how much the work of a small group of dedicated young men.

Off-campus experience has a different quality, and probably different educational meaning for students, depending on the general character or climate of the institution, and the orientation of its professors. At Douglass College, part of the New Jersey state university, several students were involved in off-campus study that was vital to their education; but the motives of both the students and the professors were different from those at Macalester. The political scientist and the economist whose students I talked with were probably not prompted by the same sense of "service" as prompted either the Macalester students or the teachers who encouraged such interests there. The Douglass students were from the beginning vocation-minded — it was important that education should lead to a job. New York City was at their door and it would have been easy to direct them into prevocational activities. Indeed it was this possibility that prompted the interest of some of the students in off-campus studies.

But although the professors who directed such work were interested in giving concrete substance to what the students were reading and discussing in the classroom, their purposes were not to meet the vocational needs of the students. They discussed political and economic problems, and they had a "You'd better get out and see" attitude in directing some of the students into field work. It is also true that several of these students not only, later on, found jobs, but found a serious direction for work out of these experiences — a professional direction perhaps not possible without it.

The point to make here is that the vocation-mindedness was used (as the service orientation was used in the other college) for intellectual enlargement that is an academic, and not primarily a practical, gain — as, for instance the education of the student who worked in a political science course project with the Voice of America and came to grips with the problems of political propaganda in a way academic study alone would not have provided. Margaret Weaver's "field work" in the Minnesota State House is a case in point.

RESCUE FOR THE GIFTED — CREATING A SPECIAL ENVIRONMENT

Honors programs have a long history in some colleges, and, with the influx of better-prepared students from high schools, many other colleges have instituted them. What concerns both the college and the students most, in these programs, is their effect in raising academic standards, giving able students opportunity to move faster, learn more. They separate the more intelligent from the less, and they often provide more imaginative ways of educating students; although often, too, the differences are more of quantity than of kind — more books to read, more papers to write, more ground to cover. Some of the students discussing honors programs felt mainly this pressure. Some reported that the existence of an honors program raised the quality of the rest of the work in the college; but frequently both those in the honors programs and those outside them said that honors courses skim off the cream of the teaching, leaving other courses poorer; and sometimes even very able students, with an eye to the grade-point average, shunned the greater competition of honors courses.

But in a large institution honors programs not only step up the academic quality of the work students do; they create a separate, smaller, and more integrated institution within the larger, diverse one — they give some internal form to a university too many-purposed to have a single life-style.

For instance, the students in the honors program at Kansas University were freed from many of the routine requirements of the rest of the university. The seminars for these students begin with the freshman year; they cut across departmental lines; and they are taught by experienced teachers who will serve as advisers to the students, create situations that will involve them in their work, plan for them on an individual basis. Students found work in the honors courses more flexible, there was more chance to read widely, to engage in discussion — and around this program the academic life of its students centered. It was described more than once as a college within the university, and it had the effect of intensifying the students' feeling about their work (as well as perhaps improving its academic quality) that such educational enclaves always seem to have.

Sometimes the effect of such a program startles alike the students who engage in it, the faculty and administration, and the students who do not. The Scholars' Program at Brooklyn, created for a small, selected group of students, not only advanced the quality of work the students did, and gave it character, but had some general effects remarked on by students and teachers alike. This commuting college, competitive and demanding, is not noted (at least in the conversation of its students) for community spirit in intellectual matters.

The spirit of caution, competition, perhaps self-protection if not self-interest, is strong. Even a year of The Scholars' Program established a camaraderie among the students, and even with some of their teachers, for an unexpected gain, going beyond the intellectual opportunities it provided for the students. From a report on the program:

> It is interesting to see what happens to such students. . . . a few, at least, raised their heads high, sniffed the fresh breezes of freedom and found them delicious. . . .
>
> For many students The Scholars' Program was evocative of latent talent, abilities were tapped and interests were stimulated which clearly would have remained dormant — at least during this year — without the special provisions of The Scholars' Program. To cite but one example, there are two students who began the year with their mentors dubious whether they should even have been admitted to the Program; as the year closes, the mentors are predicting brilliant careers ahead for both students, who have come awake, as it were, under the mentors' guidance and challenge and demonstrated intellectual powers of the first order.
>
> For most of the faculty, working with The Scholars' Program had the effect of replacing a routine task with an experience compounded of excitement, wonderment (at the abilities and minds of some of them), and delight.

"INDEPENDENT STUDY" AND INDEPENDENT STUDY

"Independent Study" has become an educational cliché, and like other clichés has behind it a confusion of meanings. This confusion makes it difficult to keep separate the ideas and conditions that are important from those that are casual or incidental. Independent Study as a means of education has been developed for superior students even though it has always been said to be expensive; it has been proposed as a way of using "teaching resources" more efficiently; and it has been suggested as a measure of economy — "students need to spend more time learning and less being taught," is one way this has been put.

Even in times of shortage, one should not refuse to consider teaching procedures because they might be expensive — nor fear them as inferior because they are economical. Independent Study programs can be costly, and they can be economical. If we allow students who have not been prepared for it to undertake independent research, it is extremely costly, and perhaps serves the student's education less than it might at another and better-prepared time. And the effort to do this has made many teachers suspicious of the whole idea, and has frustrated many students.

But there are levels of independent study, that is, ways for students to learn, independent of the presence of the teacher — and this independent study involves reading, writing, and discussion; field work, work in the arts, and research. It involves students learning how to read, to think about what they read, to put knowledge and ideas into form, without checking up in frequent class meetings; it involves students discussing with each other, as intelligent and interested people do, what they have been engaged in learning, without the constant presence of the teacher; it involves students learning, little by little, by being given tasks and opportunities of increasing complexity, how to search out information and order it; and by all these means, in time, coming to understand what it means to be an independent student in the best sense. And this is important, because if a student does learn this he will be more likely to keep on being an independent student.

Students, even those who are not our best students, can be given a kind of independence at an early stage, and can learn from each experience. One of the things independent study requires, even on a simple, partial level, is time — that is, time for the student to discover what he is about and to go about doing it. The greatest single obstacle, not only to Independent Study programs, but to independent study without any capital letters, is the chopping up of students' work into small fragments of five or six courses: five three-credit courses, for example. On paper a student is expected to spend six hours studying for a course for which he sits in classes three hours a week. Six hours a week allows nobody to get a proper start on any independent study. However small, if it is worth the time that goes into discussing it and worth the paper it is reported on, a project needs exploring and investment — a kind of investment that cannot always be turned off after an hour and a half because something else has to be studied now. Under such circumstances students cannot be started early on independent study, and sometimes not at all. In any case they are likely to have to wait until they are seniors, when there might be more flexibility in their programs; but the difficulty then is that often they do not begin to know what they need to know in order to study independently, never having had the experience, even on a small scale. Therefore they need a great deal of supervision, and Independent Study becomes fabulously expensive.

There have been many experiments with what is called independent study, especially since about 1955 when educators started becoming seriously alarmed about the threatened shortage of teachers; a number of studies have been made of such programs. In general the evidence reported by these studies has been that students studying independently, that is, on projects or in groups without a teacher, or by being excused from regular class attendance, do not learn more than students in regular, conventional courses. This evidence tells us little or nothing about how, and how well, the students in such experiments were prepared for independent study. If they were not prepared, but were removed from a conventional kind of learning situation in a conventional kind of course, and were suddenly confronted with a demand for an entirely new kind of learning, the research may still leave unexplored both the problems and possibilities of independent learning which affect the students, the teacher, and the subject of study.

A study based on review of many Independent Study programs,* reports that the chief objection of teachers to such programs is the burden placed on them. And since in many instances supervising independent study is a task added to regular teaching loads, it must become a burden. This superimposing of what should be a good way of teaching and learning on an already designed curriculum reflects the reluctance of administrators, department heads, and teachers themselves, to eliminate any of the courses in their departments. If teachers taught fewer courses and students "took" fewer, this burden would be lifted. The usual objection to this idea is that the students need all the listed courses in order to "cover" the subject, and this view prolongs the fallacious notion that knowledge comes by studying particular segments in particular units of time.

Teachers are also reluctant to supervise independent study, according to this account, unless it is in the field of their own scholarly research; and this reluctance can be understood when one remembers that it is the volume of published research for which teachers are first rewarded by their institutions, not for either the volume or the quality of their teaching.

* *The Independent Study Program in the United States,* J. Carver Drushal and Associates, New York, Columbia University Press, 1957.

Both teachers and students found serious objections to independent study plans in the "lack of sufficient guidance, the possibility of procrastination, the feeling that the program is not so demanding or rewarding as course work, the insufficient amount of time or credit allowed for the program, limited library and laboratory facilities, and loss of valuable courses." All these troubles, with the exception of the inadequacy of library and laboratory facilities have to do, not with what independent study can be, but with failures in the way it is designed and administered.

In spite of these limitations, both teachers and students found twice as many assets as drawbacks in independent study, and what the students valued most was "the chance to learn to work resourcefully or creatively on ones' own." And this indeed is the object of education, not only of independent study.

Teachers recognized in such teaching an opportunity to broaden their own knowledge of their fields, and it was thus intellectually stimulating to them. Some teachers, who had no other opportunity for close contact with students, valued this part of it, and valued the sense of helping students develop scholarly interest and competence, and the opportunity to evaluate students' educational needs and accomplishments.

But this is not the place for the analysis of either Independent Study as an educational device, or independent study as a way for students to learn. It is necessary to comment on the experience of students in this book with independent study as it affected their involvement in their work.

Although nobody initially announced it as a principle, the expectation that students would learn to work independently shows up in all three of the freshman programs I described earlier, and deliberate efforts to help them learn were built into all the programs. At The New College, after the morning lecture, students were expected to spend time working at the questions raised there, and they had the rest of the morning free to do it. The Fellows soon found they had to make some readjustments; students were not able to carry on systematic and intensive study in a new field without help. Developing capacity to do this was not regarded merely as a hurdle which students were expected to leap somehow, but as a barrier to studying independently which they had to learn to surmount as quickly as possible. The faculty made it part of the design of that program to give students such help in the beginning so they would need it less later on. "By the end of the year most of them had developed self-discipline, and were able to discuss academic subjects in ways superior to the average college freshman."

Another kind of help toward independence is described by a faculty member at Sarah Lawrence College. The importance of immediately beginning work that leads both to self-understanding and independence is central to the Sarah Lawrence program. Genuine independence involves discovering work to do — subjects to study, ideas to explore, attitudes to discriminate — that are important to one's developing intellectual life, as well as procedures and techniques to follow. And it is this view that has governed the decision that from the beginning, learning in these terms should be made possible:

> This is quite different from honors work in the junior and senior years and serves a wholly different purpose. These freshman courses help a student develop her own sense of direction. Darwin said of Professor Henslow with whom he took long exploratory walks, more important to him than any of his university courses, "He helped me to become myself, to know who I am." Such a course also helps the student to realize the demands of subject matter. She cannot follow her own interests whimsically. She has to develop that kind of discipline that means learning to do what you *have* to do in order to do what you *want* to do.

It is the first lesson in independent study, and should begin early. Unfortunately most Independent Study programs are "reserved" for students who are judged by faculty to have, one way or another, developed the capacity, by the time they are advanced in their college work, to do it. Sometimes the faculty judgment is correct; often it develops that the student cannot study independently, and the process of the student's work takes an inordinate amount of faculty time teaching him things he should have learned before undertaking independent study.

The Scholars' Program at Brooklyn, in its brief existence — it was begun in 1961 — has dealt forthrightly with some of the most obvious bars to independent study — the practical as well as educational ones. They have cut through the traditional course-credit problems by deciding that work of a student, when it is part of The Scholars Program will be recorded so that the credit rating "instead of being fixed as is the case for regular courses, will vary with the work done by the student."

It has been the purpose of this program to give students the encouragement to "take increasing responsibility for their own education;

the role of the faculty member involved (becomes) that of catalyst, guide, or resource for occasional conference."

Students worked alone in the research laboratory, two together in the genetics laboratory; a chemistry student worked independently through the introductory and quantitative analysis course.

In the late 1950's a group of imaginative people dreamed up a plan for a new college that would draw on the resources of four established institutions, but would have its own character, its own curriculum, meet the demands of the parent colleges in its own way.* The central feature of the college plan was to introduce students to ways of studying designed to engage them in the process and to develop from the beginning a way of working independently, as educated adults need to work.

This college never came to life, but in the year some of the students in this book came to college the men who created the idea of that college put some of its hopes and ideas into practice in the existing colleges. For one year some seminars for freshmen and for seniors were conducted at the four colleges as a modest demonstration of the bold college plan. This project, like the original one, was a creative effort "to deal with the intellectual lassitude that has been the object of so much concern." It is described as a project "aimed at countering the tendency of our undergraduates to leave too much of the initiative in their education in the hands of their teachers." It might as justly have been described as an effort to remove the tendency of teachers and courses to keep initiative out of the hands of students:

> We provided that instead of first encountering broad surveys of the results of scholarly disciplines, entering students should take "Freshman Seminars" in which they should be taught how a scholar works by exploring relatively few subjects in some depth. Our Freshman Seminars are envisaged as functioning also to develop the skills of collaboration in discussion groups, with increasing opportunities for the students to take the initiative as the year progresses.

It had been the plan of the proposed Connecticut Valley college to "make student initiative and independent work the natural, expected thing, part of its style of life." A three-course program was to allow time for student projects and independent study.

* The individuals who planned this experimental program were professors at Amherst, Mt. Holyoke, Smith, and the University of Massachusetts, and the college was to have been located within reasonable commuting distance of the four parent institutions.

The freshman seminar, adopted from the abandoned plan, and tried out in the parent colleges, met once a week instead of three or four times, as other classes did. Meetings were sometimes suspended, and the students carried on their work independently. An account of one of them says:

> The remarkable success of this seminar, to which all participants testified enthusiastically, was purchased by the instructor's daring to cut the students loose, to let them get lost, and by the students' pluck in persisting until, with the instructor's help, they found themselves. The assignments, after the first three weeks, were never specific numbers of pages in particular books. The students were given at the outset lists of classic works, monographs on the Presidency and the Congress, professional and general periodicals, documents and other sources — a list which at first seemed to them staggeringly long and in the end came to seem limited. Assignments "were made in terms of the subjects to be covered or the hypotheses to be proved. Categories of material were referred to as the probable 'best sources' to use."
>
> The instructor reports that "this do-it-yourself . . . at first caused a goodly amount of floundering about" and she indicates that another time she would offer more aid at the outset. She reports also that this kind of learning "does take time . . . students need to rummage around in books and materials, to make mistakes in selecting books and materials, to find the better materials."
>
> But the investment of time and nerves was clearly worth it, for the students all testify to having gained a new kind of interest in the work and confidence in their own powers.

Students had to read, to think about questions, to bring back, in discussion and papers the results of their reading and thinking. These courses had the defects of their virtues — discussion was often not to the obvious point, students confused accidental with central issues.

"This type of course, in contrast to the standard ones," one teacher reported, "reveals the measure of the student's mind, what needs to be done to develop it, and whether or not a student is or is not making progress in the subject":

> That the students appreciated those features of the course which required them to exercise their own minds to learn for themselves . . . is most heartening and heart-warming.

Another adaptation of the new college plan was the creation of student-run seminars and discussion groups for seniors. These, like the freshman seminars, required students to participate in the whole design of their study, and taught them how to work independently. Perhaps in this connection an important comment to make is the insight such teaching gave teachers about *their* work, as well as students about theirs.

One participant, an experienced teacher reflecting on his experience with the discussion groups, spoke of the realization that:

> in classroom teaching, less gets across by my tone than I had thought. Not that you should give up the habit of speaking freely, from your own vantage. But I had a revelation of some self-deception in teaching. I realized that I sometimes sophisticated myself out of what for the students was the heart of the matter. They opened it up. For me it was a marvelous experience; it took the top of teacher's head off.

Such an experimental program, creating for students a way of working in only a small part of their studying life, embedded in a conventional curriculum, can have limited impact. It is described here because it illustrates what was intended to be the design of a whole "satellite" college. Student reports of this project show that even in this partial form it gave new impetus to their work, and they drew energy from it as they always do from imaginative and self-propelling programs.

But for all the talk about Independent Study programs, apart from these special programs, there was, in the small sample of institutions whose students are in this book, little indication that developing the capacity to work independently, in any major way, was a basic purpose, or part of the animating principle of the institutions themselves. In some instances students wrested the chance from the college; in some, individual professors saw to it that individual students had such opportunities. But in general the assumption was that initiative would remain in the hands of the teacher, and that accomplishing the tasks set by the teacher, the department, the curriculum itself would be the main responsibility of the student.

XI

In Support of Decentralizing: Satellite Colleges

THE present pressure of students to enter colleges increases both the possibilities and the hazards of education in our time — it gives us a chance to redesign education, and presents the danger of trying to teach enormous numbers of students by means envisioned for much smaller numbers. Whether it is literally true, as somebody reported in the hallway discussions at an educational conference in the fall of 1963, that, at a great middle-western university two thousand more students had registered that fall than had been anticipated, the story is a reminder of what confronts us. It is also significant that a few weeks later the president of that university expressed interest in the possibility of dividing his institution up into colleges of five or six thousand students each.

As numbers increase, academic standards at least in some institutions, go up. "We don't have to take anyone with less than 700 in the College Entrance Examination scores," says the admissions director of a selective college. And although such a comment is usually accompanied by assurances that other criteria are also important, reports on incoming students indicate that many students apparently also meet the other criteria, whatever they may be, because scores are very high.

The race for high scores, for more National Merit Scholars, and for others winning national scholarships, among colleges which never had such opportunity for selecting students, will fix more and more attention on such criteria. But higher examination scores will not deal with indifference, the lack of serious involvement in the enterprise; these difficulties have been found often enough on campuses where the admissions scores are high to make it clear that such standards themselves do not bring commitment to intellectual values with them.

Moreover we will not in any case fill our colleges with high-scoring, highly motivated students; and indeed with increasing numbers will come greater anonymity and greater detachment. In the midst of centralization and growing bigger, we need to have decentralization, and by that means grow smaller.

Colleges and universities try to protect the students they consider most gifted by honors courses and other special programs. But this is not good enough.

We need to use all the devices being developed, as they demonstrate what they can contribute to education, for the education of large numbers of students. Television and teaching machines will accomplish important things; but the increasing anonymity of students will not accomplish what the serious relation of teachers to students and of students to each other will accomplish.

And so we need to create ways of educating students, not just those few "best" ones, that will make it possible for them to work and think and talk with each other, and with teachers.

In every instance the creation of new colleges, or special programs within colleges, that make it possible for such communication to take place, has heightened learning and pleasure in learning. Some of these examples, and students' response to them have been discussed here.

The seminars at Harvard of which Scott Hansen was a part accomplished this to a high degree for the kind of students who were accepted at Harvard; The New College, which provided a more complete experience for its students, accomplished it to a high degree for students as unmotivated as Alex Rovere was when he came, as well as for the students more obviously ready to make use of a new and demanding educational experience.

In the 1930's and earlier, whole new experimental colleges were established to create the environment that minimizes indifference, makes attachment to the experiences of learning a natural thing.

The strength of the associations among students and with teachers and for learning in such places lasts long — outlives the institution itself, sometimes. Alexander Meiklejohn's Experimental College in Wisconsin lasted only five years (it is hard to believe it) but that college is not only still a force in the lives of people who experienced it; its name and its example rise up even today in any discussion of creative educational design.

It is unlikely that in these days of costly facilities it will be possible to create many new small independent institutions now.

What we can do is to create satellite colleges, attached to already existing institutions, that will provide the place, the ways of learning, the relationships between teachers and students, the life-style and the high expectations that will draw out of students that energy, imagination, and will that makes education a living experience and not a matter of form.

Such enclaves, satellite colleges, should be created on or near the campus of an established college or university for groups of students —

two hundred or five hundred or maybe more, depending on the size of the parent institution — students acceptable for admission to the institution itself. They should not be honors colleges; they should admit the same kind of students who are admitted to the parent college or university; they should have the same faculty-student ratio as the parent institution. They should be designed by teachers interested in creating an educational design or style, who would try out, for whatever population the college has, educational ideas and methods created by experimental institutions under the favorable conditions that made experimentation freely possible, and so test such ideas under present conditions; they should invent their own new ways with knowledge, appropriate for their students and these times.

Such a satellite college should have its own faculty and its own classrooms — the structure of the curriculum, the number of courses each student takes, the scheduling of classes, might be entirely different in the satellite and the parent, and teachers should not divide their energies or their loyalties between two systems or be forced to shift the rhythm of their teaching. Teaching in institutions or programs that set out to engage the students, and not merely pass on the teacher's wisdom for whatever the students can make of it, is time-consuming and energy-consuming. Students should study few things at once, and teachers should teach few courses at once. And perhaps teachers should every few years have a change of pace, and teach for a while in the less demanding atmosphere of the parent institution.

Located on or near the campus of the parent institution, the satellite should use the facilities of the parent that are most costly — science laboratories and the library, for example; if the students were not in the satellite college they would be in the parent institution, and using its facilities. A satellite college can get along with a minimum of administrative personnel — the registrar, the bursar, and the other officers of management in the parent institution would in any case have to deal with the records of their students if they entered regularly into the parent institution.

The satellite should have a limited curriculum, and teach with distinction those subjects it teaches. It could use, for its own purposes, television lectures or other large-scale educational enterprises on the parent campus; but the heart of the students' education should be its own program. That program should not be unreasonably confined, but neither should it offer the large array of courses that have come to be thought the common and necessary fare of undergraduate education. It does not matter if the student does not study everything. It will be a cause for rejoicing if he learns some significant things and emerges with the habit of learning. Branches of a big university, distributed around the state, that merely duplicate the university's curriculum, or all the required courses of the first two years, will not do.

Satellite colleges surrounding a main university or college could create a curriculum and design ways of studying that would leave the main institution undisturbed; and should be more easily brought into existence by creative teachers than changes in the main body which might threaten the Establishment. The university itself could go its way undisturbed.

A conspicuous lack in the education of students I talked with was any firsthand experience with the arts, and particularly the visual arts. They studied the history of art, aesthetics, even the psychology of art, in some places; but they never entered a studio or handled a brush. In most colleges the practice of an art is not part of a liberal education, except for fine arts majors, and often not much for them. A satellite college somewhere could try, as one part of its curriculum, giving students opportunity for work in a studio as students in most places are given an opportunity for work in laboratories; not for the education of fine arts majors, but to enable students of literature or history or science to learn how to see as an artist sees, as we claim we train them in research to learn how a scholar works.

Such a college might be designed to attract students to the study of science (although obviously it should not be confined to this study), but with its attention less on the graduate schools than on transmitting to students, who will live through the next half century in a physical universe of expanding possibility and power, some understanding of the revolution they are living through. Many students who study science in the ordinary course of events fail to get such education. Let us recall Bronowski's comment on that subject quoted earlier in this book.

A satellite college might even develop a plan for the training of teachers that would be impossible to institute in the major institution, or create a curriculum giving students much larger opportunities for off-campus studies than could be fitted into the curriculum or the schedule of the parent.

It might even deal with the compulsion of grades. The Harvard seminars are ungraded, and their ungradedness has been recognized by the students, the faculty who teach them and, by now, even by others, as an important force in the students' involvement in the work itself. A few colleges in the country have avoided using grades, not choosing to hide the complexity of the educational experience, and the complexity of judging it, under the specious simplicity of letters or numbers. But this practice is not likely to grow.

Serious students often talked about how the grading system influenced what they studied — the need to keep the grade-point average high for scholarship or graduate-school purposes — and the fact that they felt they could rarely take the risk of studying something they might do badly by the prevailing standards, when they could study something they knew they could do well. "Leading from strength," Riesman points out, "may rob the students of the possibility of discovering other areas in which they may not be so well-equipped, but which may nevertheless be more relevant for them as they slowly grow."

It might be possible for a small satellite college to devise other ways of evaluating the work of its students that would be a stimulus to their study, but would not be possible in a large institution. And, as with the rest of the experiments it could make, it might provide not models, perhaps, but suggestions for the parent institution to follow.

A report by an exceptionally forthright administrator at a college with high academic standards states the case:

> What had the college actually done for the 54 scholastically most gifted students in the class under discussion? It had intended to provide the opportunity to develop intellectually and culturally and had offered basic knowledge and methods of research by means of which they would be able in the future to continue their studies independently. But only about 25% of this group had matured into self-directing, intellectually curious human beings who seemed capable of creative effort. The rest had achieved excellent grades, had even graduated with honors, but although they were driven by ambition, they were circumscribed in their accomplishments by a misunderstanding of educational aims, by an unwillingness to break the shell of conformity, and by a belief that good grades obtained by choosing the right courses and taking the correct attitudes must ultimately lead to success — attitudes for which exterior circumstances, not the students themselves, are mainly responsible.

Not once but often teachers (if they are conscientious and thoughtful enough) face with a heavy heart not the "flunker" but the glib, facile "A" student. Well these teachers know that the process whereby the glib "A" student acquired the "A" empties the term education of all meaning whatsoever. Yet, how to deny the student his "A" grade?

These students, whether they were ever conscious of it or not, experienced exactly the educational loss described in the "Harvard Freshman Seminar Report" when it speaks of the Harvard student who, "sometimes for four 'creditable' years" is able safely to disregard the basic expectation of that great university that he "reflect on his beliefs and criticize his suppositions." The seminars were created to make such reflection and criticism central to his education.

Perhaps by a more searching exploration of some of the conditions under which education *does* help students become "self-directing, intellectually curious human beings . . . capable of creative effort," we can cut down the loss.

A satellite college might even be a "partial" college — the first two years, providing a curriculum with its own design, the main institution agreeing to adjust its requirements where necessary, the students who have had two years of the new institution also taking some risks in meeting the later requirements of the parent institution. If there is flexibility on the part of the parent, there can safely be risks on the part of the students. Students at The New College who were part of this study had an absolutely different first-year curriculum from those at Hofstra, the parent university, but they moved from one to the other without jeopardy, often with a year and a half of acceptable credit for a long year and a summer's work. And their records for the final years at Hofstra are good.

There are some things that all the students interviewed for this study, whether they were students with the high College Board scores at Harvard, the students of Brooklyn College with superior high school records, the "good average" students of The New College, or the students at any of three state universities; whether they came from a woman's college like Spelman or one like Sarah Lawrence — there were some things all of them, all these students for whom their studies were important to their lives, wanted; valued when they had them, resented it when they did not.

They sought and cherished serious intellectual communication with a teacher; recognition by a teacher of what their minds were engaged in. They did not expect or even want to have this kind of relation on all occasions; for some it never had, and did not need to have, a

deeply personal quality; but they resented indifference and forced anonymity. Alex Rovere was immediately visible to teachers because his
work was sufficiently concentrated in content, in time, and place, for
teachers to see what was happening to him.

They wanted time. In almost every instance when students were
involved in studying five things at once, they described how they slighted
one or two, worked to get by, chose carefully, often with the skillful advice of friends, one or two courses where work could be done as a matter
of form, so they could make time for studying something else; or they
described how the struggle to do too many things in too little time
meant that nothing was done quite well. At The New College students
studied only two subjects at one time — one general course lasting
through the year for all students, a second, intensive course changing
twice in the course of the year. At Sarah Lawrence students have always worked in three courses at once. Certain of the Harvard Seminars
required a particular humanities course to be taken at the time of the
seminars, the two supplementing each other, and occupying half the
student's time. All these ways meant for the students a chance to work
seriously, and in depth, from the beginning.

They wanted time, and the chance to talk about their work, not
only in bull sessions around the cafeteria table, but in class; when they
had worked and thought about their work, they wanted to communicate, to listen, to find out how their ideas sounded when they were
spoken aloud.

They wanted chances to use initiative, to discover their own ways
of functioning. Margaret Weaver took the matter into her own hands, as
her story indicates, and her college went along.

They did not wish isolation — no more in relation to their work
than in relation to their personal lives. This is no wish for togetherness,
or warmth out of anxiety, or associations that will enable them to hide,
although surely many students seek that kind of escape from isolation.
But many accept that kind of escape because they find none in the design or organization of their studies, their working relation to teachers
or other students. Where they have been given fair chance to establish
identification with the part of their life given to study, most of them
have used it.

The accounts of individual students, of programs calculated to
enlist the student's energies, to engage him in his studies, illustrate some
ways in which these ends have been sought by both students and insti-

tutions. Creating separate educational units, satellites of existing institutions, each with its own life, and character, can intensify the involvement of students, deal creatively with increasing numbers, and, perhaps, teach us something about ways of education.

These years are seeking years. Young people of college age are more conscious of their possibilities than they were in their earlier years. However they flounder, they are trying to find out how to use life and what to live for. Hostility, indifference, the inability to commit themselves to action or to intellectual experience, the tendency to herd together on a level of semi-consciousness are seen by their own testimony to be a cover for a failure in the search to find some positive direction. This failure, and the retreat that follows upon it may be beyond our help. The world they were born into, the disillusionment or unconcern of the families they grew up in, may make it impossible for them to live in positive and creative ways, and they may be bound to settle for such self-guarding safety as they can find. They are in a state of unsettledness and change. If we accept the view that they are inaccessible to us, we become custodians only and accept a feeble role for education. If we cannot, with the dramatic stuff of literature and science, anthropology and politics, art and social thought, direct students out of their floundering into commitment instead of retreat, we have accepted the view that, save for the already-committed few, education has only a practical, vocational, or status usefulness. In American colleges we are not teaching highly developed, intellectually dedicated young people; but neither are we teaching disillusioned and defeated adults. They do not like defeat and they do not like to withdraw.

Teachers often assume that exhorting students, or exposing them to great ideas assures that they will adopt great ideas. What, in fact, do we do to "induce" students to "re-examine their established ways and accepted habits of thought"? How wise or interested are we in appealing to those impulses in them that are precisely what we need to reach if we are to have them not only hear what we say but question what they feel, or believe, or think? We have plenty of evidence that exposure to college for four years does not itself accomplish this, and instead of being worried about the students only, we have reason to question whether in some way the "exposure" cannot be made more fruitful. If there is reason for students to be in college, and if they remain substantially unaffected by the intellectual, personal, and social values liberal education is intended to promote, it is everybody's failure.